PARTY CAKES

50 Spectacular Cakes To Make, Ice & Decorate

PARTY CAKES

50 Spectacular Cakes To Make, Ice & Decorate

Virginia Welsh & Alison French

SHELTON BOOKS

The authors and publishers would like to thank Guy Paul and Company Ltd for their
food colourings and David Mellor, 26 James Street, Covent Garden, London and Covent
Garden Kitchen Supplies for lending the equipment shown on pages 8-9.

First published in 1985 by
Conran Octopus Limited
37 Shelton Street
London WC2H 9HN

Reprinted in paperback in 1992

This edition published in 1993 by Shelton Books,
an imprint of Conran Octopus Limited

Edited by Charyn Jones
Designed by Grub Street Design,
London
Photographed by Clive Corless and
Frank Farrelly
Artwork by Hussein Hussein

ISBN 1 85029 635 9

Typeset by SX Composing Ltd
Printed and bound in Hong Kong

FOREWORD

Birthday and holiday parties are often best remembered for the cake – not particularly for its taste, but how it looked. Most parents, no matter how little adept at design or icing, will try to do something special on this occasion. At The Party Place, we see parents return year after year for inspiration and ideas for their latest cake.

For this reason we decided to do this book to share some of our ideas and to show how certain effects can easily be achieved. We have aimed to keep the cakes as simple as possible and some readers may feel they can heighten an effect by adding a personal touch here and there. Some cakes are obviously more difficult in the cutting, construction and decoration, but well worth the time and effort.

Before you start, read through the main introduction at the beginning of the book. There we explain the techniques involved in cake baking and icing. We also provide some delicious cake recipes for you to try. Each cake has detailed instructions for constructing, icing and decorating it, but you should refer back to the main introduction for help with basic techniques. The templates for cutting out the shapes and decoration of the cakes are at the back of the book; some need to be sized up, others need simply to be traced off. It is very important to read the instructions for making each cake carefully and to assemble all the equipment you need before you begin. If you feel that the decoration of any particular cake is too complicated, you can, of course, always adapt it.

We hope that your children and friends will enjoy looking at the cakes in this book and choosing a cake for that special occasion. Don't forget that if all else fails and your icing efforts go wrong, you can always cover the cake with Smarties or chocolate chips.

Virginia Welsh   Alison French.

CONTENTS

Festive occasions

Music and words

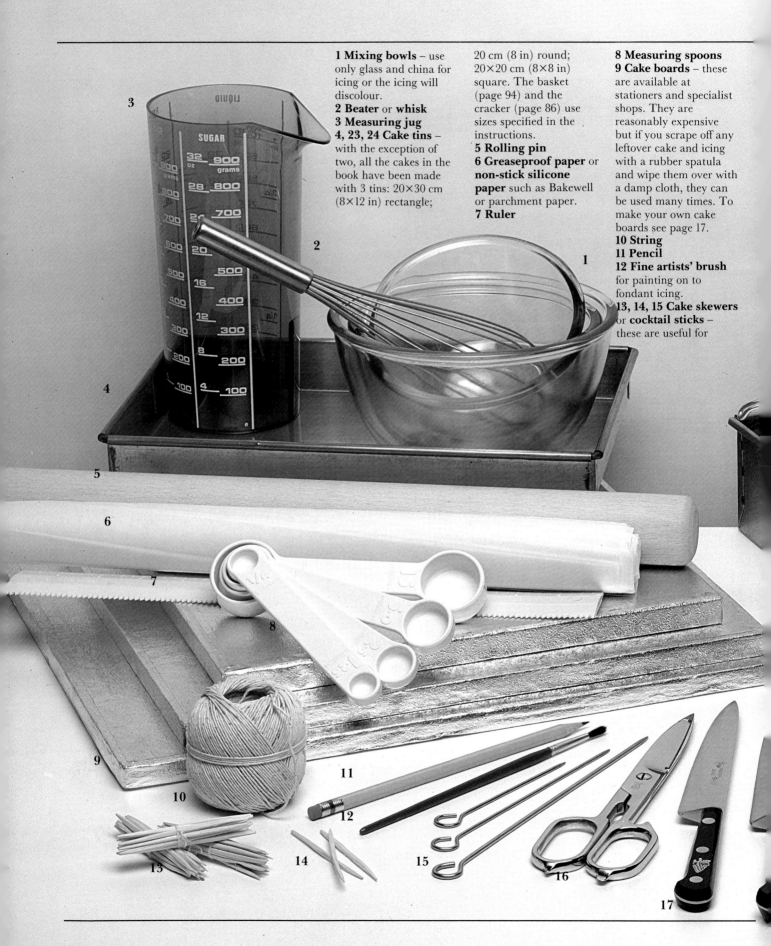

1 Mixing bowls – use only glass and china for icing or the icing will discolour.
2 Beater or **whisk**
3 Measuring jug
4, 23, 24 Cake tins – with the exception of two, all the cakes in the book have been made with 3 tins: 20×30 cm (8×12 in) rectangle; 20 cm (8 in) round; 20×20 cm (8×8 in) square. The basket (page 94) and the cracker (page 86) use sizes specified in the instructions.
5 Rolling pin
6 Greaseproof paper or **non-stick silicone paper** such as Bakewell or parchment paper.
7 Ruler

8 Measuring spoons
9 Cake boards – these are available at stationers and specialist shops. They are reasonably expensive but if you scrape off any leftover cake and icing with a rubber spatula and wipe them over with a damp cloth, they can be used many times. To make your own cake boards see page 17.
10 String
11 Pencil
12 Fine artists' brush for painting on to fondant icing.
13, 14, 15 Cake skewers or **cocktail sticks** – these are useful for

KITCHEN TOOLS AND EQUIPMENT

holding the template firmly on the cake, for transferring designs and making decorations.
16 Kitchen scissors
17 Sharp knives
18, 20 Palette knives – short- and long-bladed knives are essential for flat icing and smoothing a cake with butter icing.
19 Wooden spoon

21 Icing bag and **tubes**
22 Stainless steel aspic cutters in small and medium sizes – these are useful for making shapes

out of fondant icing and for leaves and other decorations.
25 Sieve

Piping tubes

These are available made from plastic or metal. There are some icing sets that screw on to the end of a metal syringe. These are, however, more difficult to control and we recommend icing bags. The tubes can then either be inserted directly into the bag or attached by means of a screw adaptor which enables you to change tubes without emptying the bag of icing. The connector goes into the bag and the tubes are attached on to the outside of the bag by means of a screw-on collar. We have used fine, medium and thick writers, 5-point star, ribbing, ribbon, frill and basket base tubes.

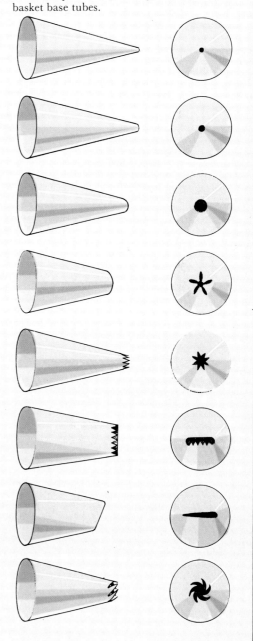

MAKING THE CAKES

The mixture for most of the cakes in this book is a basic butter sponge – the traditional Victoria sponge – but we have included an all-in-one sponge that is quick and easy to make. You can use your own favourite recipe or one from a packet provided it makes the quantity needed for each cake. If you check on the flour used in your cake and then adapt it to use 225 g (8 oz) of flour, that should equal one cake quantity in this book. You can flavour the mixture according to taste.

When to bake the cake
The cake should ideally be baked the day before it is iced. The sponge will then be firmer and less likely to crumble when you cut out the shape and ice it. You can make it a month beforehand and keep it in the freezer in an airtight bag. Allow 12 hours to thaw in the refrigerator, still in its airtight bag, before using. If you can't bake the cake in advance, allow it to cool and then place it in an airtight bag in the freezer for 1-2 hours to firm it up. Apricot glaze is essential on a fresh cake to stop the crumbs from getting into the icing (see page 12).

The cake mixture
In the instructions for the icing and decorating of each cake in this book, we state the number of cake mixtures required. The recipes here are equal to one mixture. For best results, have all your ingredients at room temperature which means removing milk, eggs and butter or margarine from the fridge at least an hour before using.

Preparing the tins
You can either line your tin with non-stick paper (Bakewell or parchment) or greaseproof paper or grease it with softened butter. If you use non-stick paper, place the tin on the paper, draw around it and cut out the shape. Place the paper in the bottom of the tin. This helps the cake to come out easily. You can also line the sides with non-stick paper if you want to. To grease the tin, melt the butter and brush all over the cake tin with a pastry brush, making sure you get into the corners. You could use a piece of kitchen towel if you have no brush. After greasing the tin, dust with flour and shake off excess. It is safer to grease or line non-stick tins too.

Baking the cake
Unless otherwise stated place all cakes in the oven so that the top of the cake is as near the centre as possible. Always test the cake for readiness (see below); cooking time may vary depending on the individual oven.

To test if the cake is cooked
To test small cakes and sponges, press the top lightly with your finger. If it is firm and springs back quickly the cake is cooked. It should also have shrunk away slightly from the sides of the tin. After removing from the oven, leave the cake in the tin for 3 minutes and then run a sharp knife carefully around the sides of the tin and turn the cake out on to a wire rack to cool. The cakes, depending on whether they need a flat or raised surface for icing, should be cooled right or wrong way up; each recipe will specify this. Peel away the base paper if you lined the tin.

To test a large fruit cake, insert a warmed skewer and if it comes out clean, with no sticky, uncooked mixture on it, the cake is cooked and ready to take out of the oven.

Cutting out and marking the cake

First you must transfer the template to a piece of tissue or tracing paper (page 114). Make sure you transpose all the references on to the paper template or you will lose track of the pieces. Cut out the paper template, secure it on top of the cake and cut round it (**1**). The cake, if it was made the previous day, will not crumble and break up. Keep the paper template on top of each piece of cake and put to one side. When all the pieces are cut out, refer to the assembly instructions.

Mark the internal design lines on the cake by pricking through the lines on the tracing (**2**). The lines will eventually be covered with icing and not seen. Once the cake is flat iced with butter icing, you cannot touch the surface without spoiling it, so keep the traced shapes close by for reference for the fine details.

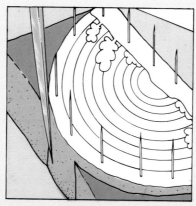

1. To cut out the shape of your cake, place the sized-up template on the top, secure it with long pins or cocktail sticks, and cut around it with a very sharp knife. Keep the template on top of the cake.

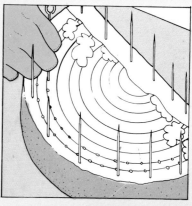

2. To transfer the outlines of the design, prick through the paper template with a skewer. If the lines are not clear enough, go over them with food colouring, or cut notches in the cake with a knife.

MAKING THE CAKES

Basic Victoria Sponge

225 g (8 oz) butter or margarine
225 g (8 oz) castor sugar
4 large eggs
6 drops vanilla essence or flavouring
225 g (8 oz) sifted self-raising flour

Preheat the oven to 325°F/160°C/Gas Mark 3 and prepare the tin. In a large mixing bowl, cream the butter and sugar until light and fluffy and pale in colour. In a separate bowl beat the eggs thoroughly then add them a little at a time to the creamed mixture, beating well after each addition. Add vanilla essence or your chosen flavouring. Gently fold in a quarter of the sifted flour; repeat until all the flour is incorporated and the mixture is smooth. Pour the mixture into a well-greased baking tin and bake for 30-35 minutes.

All-in-one sponge

225 g (8 oz) sifted self-raising flour
2×5 ml spoons (2 teaspoons) baking
    powder
4 large eggs
225 g (8 oz) soft margarine
225 g (8 oz) castor sugar
6 drops vanilla essence

Preheat the oven to 325°F/160°C/Gas Mark 3. Sift the flour and baking powder into a large bowl. Add the remaining ingredients and beat with an electric beater until thoroughly mixed. Test that the mixture drops off a wooden spoon when tapped on the edge of the bowl – if not add 1-2 5 ml spoons (teaspoons) of milk and beat again. Pour into the prepared tins and bake for 30-35 minutes.

Flavourings
To flavour either of the above recipes, omit the vanilla essence and add the following:
Coffee: Dissolve 3×5 ml spoons (3 teaspoons) of instant coffee granules with 1×15 ml spoon (1 tablespoon) of hot water and add after the flour.
Chocolate: Replace 40 g (1½ oz) flour with 40 g (1½ oz) of sifted cocoa powder.
Lemon or orange: Add the finely grated rind of the lemon or orange with 1×15 ml spoon (1 tablespoon) of the juice after the flour.
Coffee with nuts: Add 110 g (4 oz) of finely chopped walnuts to 3×5 ml spoons (3 teaspoons) of instant coffee granules dissolved in 1×15 ml spoons (1 tablespoon) of hot water after the flour.

Traditional Christmas cake

This rich fruit cake is baked in a 20×30 cm (8×12 in) cake tin.
275 g (10 oz) sultanas
250 g (9 oz) currants
250 g (9 oz) raisins
110 g (4 oz) glacé cherries
75 g (3 oz) mixed peel
75 g (3 oz) ground almonds
grated rind of 1 lemon
225 g (8 oz) sifted flour
generous pinch of salt
200 g (7 oz) butter
200 g (7 oz) dark soft brown sugar
4 eggs
4 drops of vanilla essence
2×15 ml spoons (2 tablespoons) brandy
2×5 ml spoons (2 teaspoons) mixed spice

To prepare the tin line the inside with a double layer of Bakewell paper and cut the side pieces so that they come up higher than the sides of the tin. Then tie a double layer of brown paper around the outside and tie securely with string. Preheat the oven to 300°F/150°C/Gas Mark 2. Wash and dry the fruit and cut the glacé cherries into quarters. Mix all the fruits together with the ground almonds, grated lemon rind and 1×15 ml spoon (1 tablespoon) of flour. In a very large bowl cream the butter and sugar until light and fluffy, then gradually beat in the lightly beaten eggs, vanilla essence and brandy, adding some flour with each addition. Fold in the remaining flour, spices and salt together with the fruit, add a little milk if the mixture is too dry and difficult to handle. It should, however, be a stiff mixture. Spoon into the prepared tin and slightly hollow out the centre so that it rises evenly.

Bake on a shelf below the centre of the oven for 1½ hours, then lower the heat to 275°F/140°C/Gas Mark 1 for a further 2¾-3¼ hours. Allow the cake to cool in the tin and then turn out on to a wire rack. Pierce the cake all over with a skewer and dribble brandy down the skewer into the cake. If the cake is not to be iced immediately, cool, wrap in grease-proof paper, then in foil. For good measure you can wrap it in cling film. About once every three weeks, remove and dribble more brandy over the cake.

Chocolate cake

Here is a deliciously moist chocolate cake you might like to use for the ideas in the book.
225 g (8 oz) sifted flour
275 g (10 oz) castor sugar
1×5 ml spoon (1 teaspoon) bicarbonate
    of soda
pinch of salt
50 g (2 oz) cocoa powder
2 large eggs
110 g (4 oz) soft margarine
150 ml (5 fl oz) sour cream

Preheat the oven to 325°F/160°C/Gas Mark 3. Sift the dry ingredients into a large bowl. Add the other ingredients. Beat until light and smooth. Pour into a well-greased tin, place in the centre of the oven and bake for 35-45 minutes.

MAKING THE ICING

The cakes in this book have either been decorated with butter or fondant icing or marzipan. Icing requires practice so do not be deterred if your first attempt isn't as professional as you would like.

Glazing cakes before decorating
If the cake is freshly made or if you do not feel very confident about icing, apply an apricot glaze to the cake beforehand so that crumbs do not get mixed up with the icing. If you are icing a rich fruit cake, apricot glaze helps the marzipan to stick to the cake's surface.

Apricot glaze
Sieve 2×15 ml spoons (2 tablespoons) of apricot jam into a saucepan. Add 1×15 ml spoon (1 tablespoon) of water and bring to the boil. For a sponge cake, allow to cool and brush on to the cake with a pastry brush. Apply the glaze hot to a rich fruit cake.

Basic butter icing
For best results make the icing the day it is to be used. Don't refrigerate as it will be too hard to use. If you do have to store it, butter icing will freeze satisfactorily though thaw well before using. Use the best quality icing sugar you can buy, and sieve it well. Any lumps will ruin the icing and block the tubes when you are piping on to the cake. Have all the ingredients at room temperature but if the weather is particularly hot the icing may become runny, in which case place in the refrigerator for 5-10 minutes to firm it up.

The recipe below makes 1 quantity equal to 750 g (15 tablespoons) of butter icing.

250 g (9 oz) butter or soft margarine
500 g (1.1 lb) sifted good quality icing sugar
1-2×15 ml spoons (1-2 tablespoons) milk or strained fruit juice
3-6 drops vanilla essence

Place the butter or margarine in a bowl and beat until it is very pale and soft. Continue beating, gradually adding half the icing sugar. Add the milk and then the rest of the icing sugar until the icing is smooth and easy to spread.

Flavourings
To flavour the icing, omit the vanilla essence and add the flavours below. Remember that you can only use coffee or chocolate flavours if you want to use brown coloured icing.
Chocolate: 3×15 ml spoons (3 tablespoons) cocoa powder mixed with a little boiling water to make a smooth paste.
Coffee: As above but substitute 6×5 ml (6 teaspoons) instant coffee granules or beat in 6×5 ml (6 teaspoons) instant coffee powder.
Orange or lemon: Add the finely grated rind of an orange or lemon together with 2×5 ml spoons (2 teaspoons) of the strained juice. Remember, if you are piping with a fine tube, strain the fruit juice well and omit the rind; it will block the tube.
Liqueur: Replace the milk or fruit juice with any liqueur.

Colouring
Basic butter icing should be pale creamy-yellow. To colour it, place the required amount of icing in a china or glass bowl and add liquid food colouring by dipping in a skewer and allowing the colour to drip into the icing (**3**). Blend evenly throughout (**4**). Add only a little at a time to achieve the right effect. You will then see how much colour you need to add. If you are using a paste colour, use a cocktail stick, skewer or the end of a spoon to add the colouring. Colours take 15-20 minutes to darken, so you might like to wait and then check it again. You can always add more colour to the icing but it is difficult to lighten a colour. If you are using strong colours, such as black or red, you may like to add a flavouring to mask the taste given by

the extra colouring. Before you start using the icing, make sure you have made enough icing. It is difficult to duplicate the exact shade.

Take care when working with food colouring; it marks everything – your hands, the work surface and clothes.

Food colouring names
We have used colours from Cake-time throughout this book with the exception of the Christmas red, silver and gold, which come from Mary Ford. The names these companies give to their colours will be

3. Mix colour into the icing drop by drop, using a skewer as a dip stick. You can always darken the icing but it is difficult to lighten a colour.

4. You can blend colour into icing with a small palette knife (or into fondant icing by hand). The colour should be even throughout.

MAKING THE ICING

different from other brands, but most speak for themselves: for example, grass green or egg yellow. Some colours are more difficult to achieve, so check the photograph.

White butter icing

If you want white icing, substitute 125 g (4½ oz) of Cookeen or tasteless white cooking fat and 125 g (4½ oz) of unsalted butter for the butter or margarine in the recipe. This white colour is necessary if you want to use delicate pink, lemon or pale blue colourings.

Grey and brown icing

To achieve grey, use white butter icing and add black food colouring a little at a time until you get the correct shade. To colour icing brown, add sifted cocoa powder a little at a time. If the icing becomes too dry, add a little water to moisten it. There are brown food colourings available but they tend to be too red – more of a brick colour which is not always suitable for hair or fur.

Flat icing

When using butter icing always ice the sides of the cake first. With a palette knife (choose a size you feel happy with, a small knife gives you better control, a large one reduces the number of movements) spread the icing roughly over the sides of the cake. Place a bowl of warm water nearby, lay your hand on the top of the cake and your thumb or index finger against the edge. Dip the palette knife into the water, shake off excess water and lightly smooth the icing upwards (**5**). The water acts as a 'film' between the palette knife and the icing. The knife must be free of icing before each new sweep over the icing. You must wipe, dip and shake as you go. However, the water absorbs the colour from the icing so you can't afford to go over an area too many times -- one or two clean sweeps should be enough. The icing should be about 6 mm (¼ in) deep.

5. To flat ice the sides of a cake, place your hand on the top, and lightly smooth the icing up towards your thumb so that none goes over on to the top.

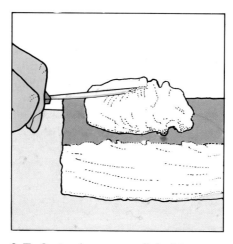

6. To flat ice the top, put all the icing you need on to the cake before smoothing it out to the sides.

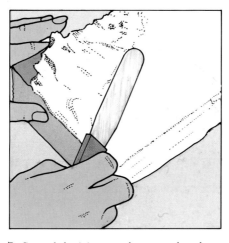

7. Spread the icing evenly out to the edges, dipping your palette knife in warm water between each movement.

To ice the top, put all the icing on to the cake (**6**) and spread it as evenly as possible to the edges (**7**). The lighter the touch, the smoother the cake will be. Do not allow the knife to touch the cake's surface or crumbs will mix with the icing. The edge where the sides meet the top will always be a problem. Smooth over it with a palette knife and pipe a line or a row of stars over the join.

Royal icing

This is usually needed for Christmas, wedding or christening cakes, and if done in the traditional way two coats and one piping coat are used, allowing time for them to dry in between. For our Christmas tree (page 98) we only used one coat. We put the icing on the cake with a wet palette knife and rough iced it to give a bushy effect. This is much quicker and easier.

The recipe below makes enough to cover a 20×30 cm (8×12 in) cake.

450 g (1 lb) icing sugar
2 egg whites
1×5 ml spoon (1 teaspoon) strained lemon juice

Roll the icing sugar with a rolling pin to get rid of any large lumps before sieving. Put the egg whites into a bowl and beat lightly with a wooden spoon. Add 2×15 ml spoons (2 tablespoons) of icing sugar and beat again. Gradually add the rest of the icing sugar, beating well between each addition until a thick consistency is obtained. Add the lemon juice and beat again. If you want a very white colour, continue beating or add 1 or 2 drops of blue food colouring. If you need a softer icing, add 1×5 ml spoon (1 teaspoon) of glycerine with the lemon juice. It prevents the icing from becoming too brittle and makes it easier to cut.

BUTTER ICING

8. To make an icing bag, form a paper cone by rolling 2 corners of a triangle to meet the 90° corner.

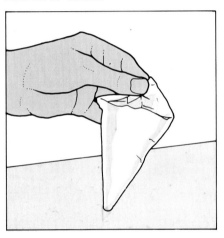

9. To prevent any icing escaping from the bag, fold in from both sides and fold the top down again.

10. To squeeze out the icing through the hole, curl your fingers over the top of the bag and use the ball of your hand and your fingers to exert pressure.

Icing bags and attachments

Nylon icing bags are probably the simplest to use. They are sold in several sizes and are easily cleaned. It is wise to have more than one bag, especially if you are using several colours on a cake. We have specified the desired number of icing bags in each recipe, but one icing bag would do, though you would need to wash and dry it between each colour.

Making your own bag

Cut out a square of greaseproof or non-stick silicone paper, fold it diagonally and cut out along the fold-line to make a triangle. Take the two 45° angles, and roll them round to meet the 90° angle making a perfect cone with no hole at the point (**8**). Secure the bag where the edges meet with a stapler or a piece of waterproof tape. Put the icing into the bag, fold down the top edges (**9**) and snip a very small hole at the end. Gently push the icing down towards the hole and only enlarge the hole when you have tested the thickness of the icing line it makes. These small homemade bags are better for fine work, so don't make them too large. You will, of course, have to make a new one each time you change the colour of the icing.

Filling and holding the bag

Insert the piping tube and drop the spoonful of icing into the bag. Never fill an icing bag more than half full as the icing may ooze out of the top. Fold in first one corner, then the other and fold the top over by about one quarter of the depth of the bag (**9**). Experienced cake decorators have different holds on the bag but the important thing is to curl your fingers around the top of the bag to stop the mixture oozing out, with the twisted end between your thumb and index finger (**10**). This will cause the icing to move down into the tip each time you squeeze. The pressure comes from your fingers and the ball of your hand. As you

decorate, twist the top of the bag further down, forcing the icing into the tube. If necessary, use the other hand to guide the bag. Practise as much as possible, piping on to a plate so you can reuse the icing.

Decorative techniques with butter icing

Making stars or 'rosettes'

The entire cake or just one area can be covered with icing stars. The stars should be very close together so that no cake is visible between them. Using the star tube, hold the bag upright with the point of the tube about 2 mm (⅛ in) from the cake and squeeze until the star is formed, release the pressure on the icing bag and pull the tip of the tube away. After you have done one row of stars close together, the next row should fit in between the stars of the previous row (**11**). To ice an entire cake in this way, take a line to start with, whether it is part of the design or just from one side of the cake to the other, and pipe your first row to give you a starting point for the rest of the rows. When making stars with a star tube, we have used our own verb 'rosette' throughout the book.

Writing or piping a line

To pipe a line you should hold the bag at 45° and touch the tip of the tube on to your surface. Begin to squeeze and at the same time raise the tip slightly so that the icing is partly suspended. It will flow out as you guide it along your line (**12**). To end the line, stop squeezing and touch the tube back on to the surface and pull away.

Transferring a written message to the cake

If the message is to go on fondant icing, practise writing it out, and when you are confident, write it on a piece of tracing paper. Place the tracing on the cake and prick

BUTTER ICING

through the letters with a cocktail stick. If the letters are to go on butter icing, you will have to write the message freehand. For both types of icing, practise icing the message first on paper or a plate (**13**). Choose the writer tube depending on how thick you want the lettering.

Ribbing and basket weave effects
The technique for using the tubes to achieve these special effects is just the same as that used for piping a line. It is important to keep the pressure on your icing bag constant so that you do not get sudden splurges or widened lines. Only practise will help you to achieve this. To obtain the ribbed effect, make sure that you pipe the lines very close together so that no cake is visible between them. To achieve the basket weave effect, start by piping a series of parallel vertical lines. The trick is to make sure that the space between your vertical lines is the same width as the lines made up by the icing from the wider tube. Then, having changed the tube to make wider flatter lines, pipe broken horizontal lines, going over one vertical and stopping before the next (**14**).

Icing direct from a tube
If you are only icing a small part of the design, such as a dot on a cat's nose, you can put the icing straight into the tube (**15**) and press with your thumb or finger (**16**). This means you don't have to use a bag for a small job.

Candle rosettes
You can make candle holders out of butter icing. Pipe a large star directly on to the cake board or onto the cake itself and insert the candle.

Extending the theme
You can ice directly on to the cake board if you want to extend the theme. You should use a cake board 10-15 cm (4-6 in) larger all round than the cake.

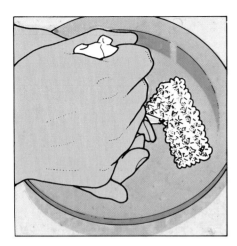

11. To cover an area with rosettes, first make one row of stars, and then rosette a second row in between those stars so no cake is visible between the stars.

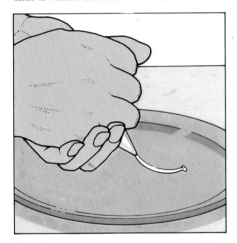

12. When piping a line, raise the tip of the bag above your working surface and touch down at the end of each completed stroke.

13. You should practise piping your message on a piece of paper or a plate before you attempt to pipe it on the cake.

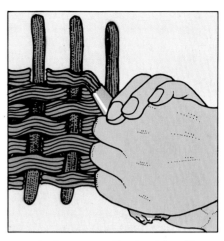

14. A basket weave effect is achieved by piping flatter, wider horizontal lines over alternate vertical lines. You will need 2 different tubes for this.

15. To make the rosette or dot with the tube, you should press into it with your thumb or finger.

16. To ice very small parts of the design, you need not use the icing bag, but can ice directly from the tube.

FONDANT AND MARZIPAN

Fondant Icing

This is sometimes called moulding icing and it is easy to work with. You can roll it out and either completely cover a cake with it, or use it cut into shapes for decoration or you can mould it into flowers, figures or animals. You can also paint directly on to it using food colouring. Fondant will keep for some time if stored in an airtight bag in a cool place.

The recipe below makes 450 g (1 lb) or 9 tablespoons of icing.

450 g (1 lb) icing sugar
1 egg white
50 g (2 oz) liquid glucose (available from most large chemists)

Sift the icing sugar into a bowl. Make a well in the centre and add the egg white and liquid glucose. Beat with a wooden spoon, collecting all the icing sugar from the edges of the bowl. Knead the icing with your hands, as you would bread dough, mixing in the remaining icing sugar at the same time. Knead until you have a soft pliable icing.

Marzipan

If you don't want to bother making fondant icing, you can use commercially prepared marzipan for the decoration in most of the recipes in this book. Marzipan does not have such a smooth finish as fondant but it does take on a shape more quickly. Fondant will set firm eventually, but a free-form figure, for example, would need to be supported until it had set. Throughout the recipes we have stated whether you should use fondant or marzipan. The other major difference is that the colour of commercial marzipan is yellow and this can save colouring in some instances. However, fondant is always white, is easier to colour and gives a wonderfully professional finish.

Covering a cake with marzipan

Marzipan (almond paste) is also used to cover a cake which is to be iced with royal icing. It should be left to dry out for at least 4-7 days. The marzipan will not then stain the icing. However, if the cake is to be iced and eaten straight away, you can leave it to dry out overnight. You can make your own almond paste.

225g (8 oz) ground almonds
110 g (4 oz) icing sugar
110 g (4 oz) castor sugar
2 eggs
2-4 drops almond essence
1×5 ml spoon (1 teaspoon) lemon juice

Sift the dry ingredients. Beat the eggs with the almond essence and lemon juice and stir into the almond mixture to make a firm paste. Wrap in cling film to prevent it drying out. This amount makes 450 g (1 lb) or 9 tablespoons of almond paste.

Dust the work surface with icing sugar and roll out half the marzipan to a thickness of about 12 mm (½ in) and to a size a little larger than the area to be covered. Brush the cake with apricot glaze (page 12) and invert the cake on to the marzipan. Neaten the exposed edges (**17**) and turn the cake right side up. Brush the sides with the glaze and roll out the rest of the marzipan to the required shape and length. Roll the marzipan up for easy handling or lift it on to the cake. Press firmly (**18**) and smooth the joins with a palette knife.

Handling

Usually it is recommended that fondant and marzipan are rolled out on a board lightly sprinkled with icing sugar. We have found that using a little flour leaves less covering, and any flour remaining can be dusted off easily with a pastry brush. If you are moulding the fondant or marzipan into shapes (**19, 20** and **21**), dip your fingers in flour or icing sugar first to prevent sticking.

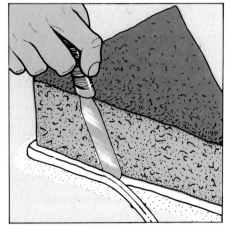

17. Neaten the exposed edges of the marzipan before lifting the cake right side up.

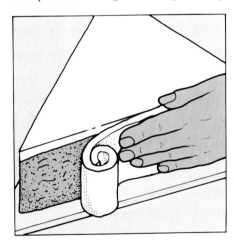

18. Cover the sides with marzipan and press firmly against the cake.

FONDANT AND MARZIPAN

19. To make a rose, curve flattened petals around a small central cone. Five petals should be enough.

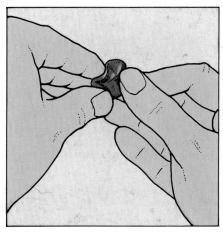

20. Gently press the center of each oval petal with your thumb to make a slight indentation.

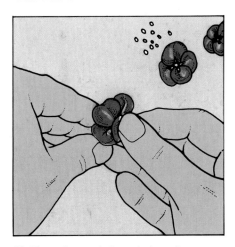

21. Place the petals in a circle to form a daisy, pinching the ends so they stay together. Roll a tiny ball of marzipan for the daisy's center.

Decorative techniques in fondant or marzipan

Colouring fondant or marzipan
Add the food colouring in drops and knead with a knife blade if you are coloring small amounts or by hand for larger quantities. Add more sifted icing sugar if necessary.

Painting fondant icing
To paint on the icing, use a fine paint brush and food colouring. Dilute the colour with egg white or water if necessary. Some food paint is not edible, silver for example, so use it only on parts that are easily removed before eating. Painting directly on to marzipan is not very successful because the marzipan is so oily.

Transferring a design
Place the tracing paper template lightly on the fondant or marzipan. With a pin, prick around the shape or lettering.

Flowers
To make a rose, take a small piece of fondant or marzipan and shape it into a cone. Take another small piece and shape it into a petal between your thumb and index finger (**19**). Curve the petal around the cone. Continue making petals – 5 is usually enough. You can add leaves if you like, either freehand or use small stainless steel aspic cutters.

To make a daisy, cut out 6-8 oval petals. With your thumb and index finger, gently pinch one end, and press the centre of each oval to form the petals (**20**). Place the petals around in a circle, pinching the ends together to join them (**21**). Using orange or yellow fondant or marzipan, roll tiny balls for the centers.

Leave fondant shapes to dry out before you use them to decorate the cake. A drop of apricot glaze will stick them on firmly.

To make your own cake boards

You can cover a baking tray, bread board, or a thick piece of cardboard with your chosen paper, either traditional silver or gold or a paper that extends the theme of your cake. The paper must have a grease-proof finish or it will absorb the butter from the icing.

The board should be 5 cm (2 in) larger all around than the cake and thick enough to hold the weight.

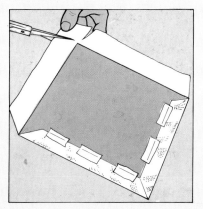

22. To cover a rectangular board, lay your paper right side down on a flat surface. Place the board on top of it. Draw a line around the outside of the board. Cut out the paper 2.5 cm (1 in) wider than the marked line. Place the board back on the wrong side of the paper, fold over the edges and secure with tape, cutting out 2.5 cm (1 in) squares at each corner for a neat flat finish.

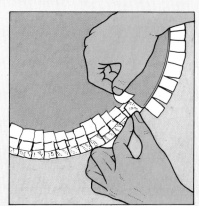

23. To cover a round board, follow the same procedure but cut into the marked line every 2.5 cm (1 in) around the circle. Fold each section over the board and tape individually.

THREE RABBITS IN BED

D★E★C★O★R★ATI★N★G
THE CAKES

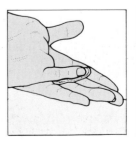

Three Rabbits in Bed, see page 39.

SOCCER GAME

Timing
1-2 hours to ice and decorate

Equipment
4 bowls for icing mixture
3 icing bags
2 tubes: star, medium writer
ruler
palette knife
cocktail stick or skewer
13 in cake board

Ingredients
1 cake, 8×12 in (page 11), cooled upside down
1 quantity of white butter icing (page 13)
food colouring: grass green, orange, red
apricot glaze (optional – page 12)

Template
page 114. Instructions for making it on page 114. Rather than scale up the template, you may like to measure directly from our template drawing and with the calculation that the lengths of the lines in centimetres are equal to the lines on the finished cake in inches, you can prick out the lines of the football pitch directly onto the cake.

Decorations
football players
posts
sandwich flags
marzipan, currant, raisin or sweet for ball

Icing the cake
Transfer the cake on to the board. Divide the butter icing into 4 bowls and colour: 1 tablespoon orange, 1 tablespoon red, 1 tablespoon white, 12 tablespoons green. Using the green icing, flat ice the top of the cake, smoothing out to the sides.

With the ruler, prick out where the lines are to go with a cocktail stick or skewer (**1**) using the illustration template as a guide. Do not let the ruler touch the iced surface. You could use a glass or biscuit cutter to mark on the centre circle (**2**). Fit the star tube to an icing bag and with the remaining green, rosette around the sides, leaving the centre 3 in on both sides for the other colours (see photograph). With clean bags, rosette on the colours in 3 bands as shown. Fit the medium writer tube to a clean icing bag and using white icing, draw in the goal mouths, perimeter lines, half-way line and corners. Start with the perimeter lines.

Decoration
Position the players and goal posts on the cake. Make a tiny football by rolling a piece of marzipan between your fingers. If you have no marzipan, use a raisin, sweet or currant. Cut sandwich flags down to size and insert in the four corners.

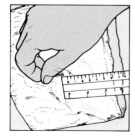

1

2

Additional ideas
You could use the colours of your favourite team on the side of the cake.

TENNIS RACKET

Timing
2-3 hours to ice and
    decorate

Equipment
5 bowls for icing mixture
4 icing bags
3 tubes: star, medium
    and thick writer
sharp knife
palette knife
cocktail stick or skewer
tracing paper
16 in cake board

Ingredients
1 cake 8×12 in (page 11),
    cooled upside down
1 quantity of white
    butter icing (page 13)
4½ tablespoons fondant
    (page 16)
food colouring: lemon
    yellow, cocoa powder,
    wood (cocoa powder
    and yellow mixed
    lightly)
apricot glaze (optional –
    page 12)

Template
page 114. Instructions for
    making it on page 114.

Decorations
plastic players (optional)

Constructing the cake
Scale up and cut out the template. Place it on the cake and cut out the three shapes. Lift the racket head and handle on to the cake board and join them together with a little of the butter icing. Using a sharp knife shave around the grip part of the handle to give a curved effect. With a cocktail stick, skewer or sharp knife, prick out the oval of the racket face where the fondant will go.

Icing the cake
Divide the butter icing into 5 bowls and colour: 1 tablespoon lemon, 3 tablespoons white, 2 tablespoons dark brown, 9 tablespoons wood. Take 1 tablespoon from the bowl of wood-coloured icing and add enough cocoa powder to it to make a dark wood colour.

Using the wood icing, flat ice the sides of the racket head and down the handle to the grip. Flat ice around the edge of the racket face, smoothing out to the edge. Roll and cut out the fondant, using the template to make the inner circle of the racket face and the triangle. Prick out the string lines with a skewer and place the fondant on top of the cake in one clean movement. Fill an icing bag fitted with a medium writer tube with dark wood icing. Following the pricked lines, pipe in the racket strings. We have woven our strings over and under one another for a realistic effect. Place the fondant triangle at the base of the racket head and pipe around it; pipe the string ends around the outside. Pipe around the edge where the top meets the side. With a clean bag, fitted with a star tube and dark brown icing, rosette the diagonal stripes on the grip. Change to white icing in a clean bag and rosette in the white stripes. Put the white icing to one side for the ball.

The ball
With a sharp knife, shape the circle to form half a ball. Put lemon icing into a clean bag fitted with a thick writer tube and pipe in the markings. Rosette the rest of the ball in white.

TENNIS RACKET

23

RUNNING SHOE

Timing
1-2 hours to ice and
  decorate

Equipment
4 bowls for icing mixture
3 icing bags
3 tubes: star, ribbing,
  fine writer
palette knife
sharp knife
tracing paper
cocktail stick or skewer
fine paint brush
13 in cake board

Ingredients
1 cake, 8×12 in (page
  11), cooled upside
  down
1 quantity of white
  butter icing page 13
food colouring: sky blue,
  sand (flesh and lemon
  yellow), orange
2 tablespoons fondant
  (page 16)
apricot glaze (optional –
  page 12)

Template
page 115. Instructions for
  making it on page 114.

Decorations
ribbon
chocolate coins for
  medals
silver food paint

24

RUNNING SHOE

Constructing the cake

Scale up and cut out the template. Place it on the cake and cut out the shape. Prick through the internal design lines with a skewer, cocktail stick or sharp knife. Shape the edge where the lace-up section is to go with a sharp knife to give a rounded edge. Lift the cake on to the board.

Icing the cake

Divide the butter icing into 4 bowls and colour: 5 tablespoons white, 4 tablespoons sky blue, 2 tablespoons orange, 4 tablespoons sand. Divide the fondant icing in half and colour one half orange. Roll out the white and the orange fondant. Using the fondant template, cut out the flash from the orange and the lace-up and top heel section from the white. Place them on the cake, curving the lace-up section round the side of the cake.

With white butter icing in a clean icing bag fitted with the ribbing tube, rib the sock from the ankle upwards in straight lines. Pipe another layer of ribbing over the top of the sock, but this time start halfway up to give the impression of a turnback on the sock. Put the white to one side.

With the sand-coloured icing, flat ice the heel piece (see photograph). Fill an icing bag fitted with a fine writer tube with the rest of the sand and pipe in the stitching on the sock turnback. This is done by piping one up and one down over the ribbing (**1**). Change to the star tube and rosette in the sole of the shoe.

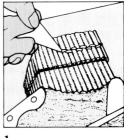

1

Fit the star tube to the white icing bag and rosette in the white sections at the toe and the back of the shoe. Using a clean bag, the star tube and sky blue icing, rosette the blue section. Finally rosette in the orange section with a clean bag and the star tube.

With a skewer, gently press into the fondant icing to make a line of stitching around the flash, the heel and the lace-up sections. Prick in small circles for eyelets. With the fine paint brush and silver paint, paint the eyelets.

Decoration

Real medals or chocolate coins can be used with ribbons for the prizes.

PLAYING CARD

Timing
1½-2 hours to ice and
    decorate

Equipment
6 bowls for icing mixture
6 icing bags
2 tubes: medium writer,
    star
palette knife
sharp knife
cocktail stick or skewer
ruler
stainless steel cutters for
    diamond or heart
    shapes
tracing paper
13 in cake board

Ingredients
1 cake, 8×12 in (page
    11), cooled upside
    down
1 quantity of white
    butter icing (page 13)
2 tablespoons fondant or
    marzipan (page 16)
food colouring:
    Christmas red, green,
    yellow, violet, cocoa
    powder
apricot glaze (optional –
    page 12)

Template
page 115. Scale up the
    template following
    instructions on page
    114. This template is
    used as a guide only.
    You may want to use
    the photograph as a
    guide.

Icing the cake
Lift the cake on to the board. Divide the
butter icing into 6 bowls and colour: 1½
tablespoons brown, 1½ tablespoons yellow,
1½ tablespoons green, 1 tablespoon violet,
1½ tablespoons Christmas red, 8
tablespoons white. With white icing, flat
ice the top of the cake, smoothing out to
the sides. Put the remainder of the white
into an icing bag fitted with a star tube
and rosette the sides of the cake. On the
edge where the top joins the sides, rosette
one row to neaten. With the ruler, prick in
a line 1 in in from the edge of the cake.
Prick in the outline of the king or queen,
using the photograph, the template or a
playing card as a guide. If possible, try to
do this profile freehand as you will then get
a neater finish. Fill a clean icing bag fitted
with a medium writer tube with brown and
pipe in the line around the outside, then
the face (it might be helpful to practise the
face on a piece of paper first) and the
crown. Change to the star tube and rosette
in the hair. In a clean bag fitted with the
medium writer tube and red icing, pipe in
the letters at opposite corners of the cake.
Change to the star tube and rosette in the
different colours of the regal robes and the
crown using a clean bag for each colour.

Decorating the cake
Colour the fondant red and roll out. Either
by hand or with heart or diamond cutters,
cut out 8 small hearts/diamonds, 2 large
hearts/diamonds and a larger heart or
diamond for the centre. In our cake the
centre of the heart has been cut away.
Position the fondant shapes on the cake.

Additional hints
If the cake is to be used for a birthday, get a
small photograph of the person and insert it
into the centre heart. The Queen of Hearts
can be used for a Valentine cake.

PLAYING CARD

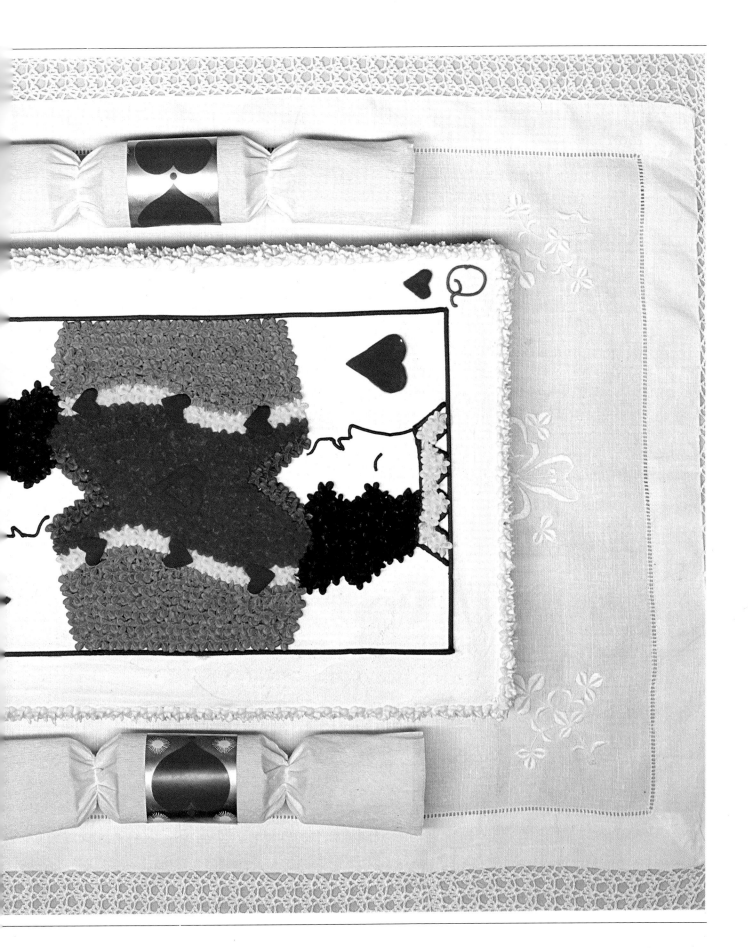

27

BACKGAMMON SET

BACKGAMMON SET

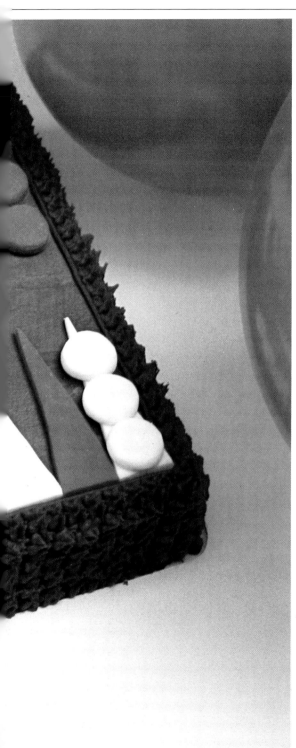

Timing
2-3 hours to ice and
   decorate

Equipment
2 bowls for icing mixture
2 icing bags
2 tubes: star, medium
   writer
palette knife
sharp knife
ruler
thin cardboard
fine paint brush
13 in cake board

Ingredients
1 cake, 8×12 in (page
   11), cooled upside
   down
1 quantity of butter icing
   (page 12)
8 tablespoons fondant
   (page 16)
food colouring:
   Christmas red, grass
   green, cocoa powder,
   black
apricot glaze (optional –
   page 12)

Template
Actual size of the
   triangles is reproduced
   below for you to trace
   on to card.

Icing the cake
Lift the cake on to the board. Divide the butter icing into 2 bowls and colour: 8 tablespoons green, 7 tablespoons brown. With green icing, flat ice the top of the cake, smoothing out to the sides. With the ruler, mark and then prick out a halfway line across the width of the cake. Put brown icing into a bag fitted with a medium writer tube and pipe a line on either side of the central line to make the two playing areas. Pipe a line around the perimeter of the cake. Change the tube to a star and rosette 2 rows in between the central lines and then rosette one row around the top and the sides of the cake.

Decorating the cake
Cut the template below in light cardboard as it is to be used several times. Colour 4 tablespoons of the fondant red and roll out the red and white fondant. Cut out 12 triangles from each colour. Try to be accurate so that they will all fit into the playing area. Place on the cake as shown in the photograph. Using the base of one of your tubes, cut out the markers – 15 white and 15 red. Position on the board.

Form the remaining white fondant into a cube for the dice and with the fine paint brush, and the red and black food colouring, paint the numbers and dots on the dice. Place the dice on the cake or the board. If you have a dice shaker, place this beside the dice. Use chocolate coins for the stakes.

3 in

⅞ in

Make a template from this triangular shape for the 24 pieces. Before cutting out the icing, check that the shape fits along either side of the cake the necessary number of times without any overlap.

PINK PIG

Timing
2-3 hours to ice and
  decorate

Equipment
3 bowls for icing mixture
3 icing bags
1 tube: star
paint brush
palette knife
sharp knife
tracing paper
13 in cake board

Ingredients
1 cake, 8×12 in (page
  11), cooled upside
  down
1 quantity of butter icing
  (page 12)
2 tablespoons fondant
  (page 16)
food colouring: rose
  pink, gold paint
apricot glaze (optional –
  page 12)

Template
page 115. Instructions for
  how to make it on page
  114.

Constructing the cake
Scale up and cut out the template. Place on
the cake and cut out the three shapes. Lift the
largest round on to the cake board.

Icing the cake
Divide the butter icing into 3 bowls and
colour: 7 tablespoons light pink, 5
tablespoons medium pink, 3 tablespoons
dark pink. Flat ice the large cake in light
pink. Put the remaining icing into a bag
fitted with the star tube and rosette the
sides. Flat ice the top of the medium round
with the medium pink and carefully place
it on to the other cake, towards the front.
With a clean bag, rosette the sides in
medium pink. Flat ice the top of the last
round in the dark pink; place it on top of
the cake towards the front as before (see
photograph). Rosette the sides of the top
piece in dark pink.

Decorating the cake
Roll out the fondant and using the
photograph as a guide, cut out 2 ears,
1 mouth, 2 trotters and 4 circles (using the
base of your tube). Roll a length for the tail
and ring. Position the pieces on the cake.
Dip the paint brush into the pink food
colouring and paint the eyes and the
inside of the ears. Clean the brush
and paint the nose ring gold.

Additional hint
This triple-tier shape could be turned into
another animal, such as a duck with a yellow
beak or a cat with a huge tail curled around it
and a 'furry' look to the icing.

PINK PIG

HORSE'S HEAD

Timing
2 hours to ice and
   decorate

Equipment
4 bowls for icing mixture
2 icing bags
4 tubes: star, ribbing,
   medium and fine
   writer
palette knife
sharp knife
cocktail stick or skewer
tracing paper
13 in cake board

Ingredients
1 cake, 8×12 in (page
   11), cooled upside
   down
1 quantity of butter icing
   (page 12)
food colouring: beige
   (egg yellow and
   brown), cocoa powder
apricot glaze (optional –
   page 12)

Template
page 116. Instructions for
   making it on page 114.

Decoration
red satin ribbon
horseshoe

Constructing the cake
Scale up and cut out the template. Place on the cake and cut out the horse shape and the extension. Mark in the internal line for the mane with a cocktail stick or make a notch with a sharp knife. Lift the two pieces of cake on to the board and join with butter icing.

Icing the cake
Divide the butter icing into 4 bowls and colour: 8 tablespoons medium brown, 4 tablespoons dark brown, 2 tablespoons beige, 1 tablespoon white. With medium brown icing, flat ice the top and sides of the cake up to the mane. Put a little white icing on the palette knife and roughly flat ice the blaze, blending over the brown as shown in the photograph. Fill an icing bag fitted with a star tube with the dark brown and rosette the mane and forelock. Change the tube to the medium writer and pipe on the nose, eye and mouth. Fill a clean bag fitted with the ribbing tube with beige and pipe on the bridle, leaving a space for the ring bit. Change to white icing in a clean bag and the medium writer tube and pipe the ring on the bit. Change to the fine writer and pipe a line decoration across the headband as illustrated. Dot white in the centre of the eye and the nostril. Smudge some white icing with the palette knife inside the ear.

Decorating the cake
Make up a red rosette by gathering up 2 lengths of red satin ribbon of different widths. Attach it to 2 straight lengths cut into a V at the ends. Add the rosette to the cake just before serving. The fat from the butter icing does seep through the satin.

KOALA BEAR

Timing
2 hours to ice and
    decorate

Equipment
3 bowls for icing mixture
2 icing bags
3 tubes: star, thick
    writer, fine writer
palette knife
sharp knife
fork
cocktail stick or skewer
tracing paper
13 in cake board

Ingredients
1 cake, 8×12 in (page
    11), cooled upside
    down
1 quantity of butter icing
    (page 12)
2 tablespoons fondant
    (page 16)
food colouring: grass
    green, black, honey
    brown (cocoa powder
    with a little yellow),
    cocoa powder
apricot glaze (optional –
    page 12)

Template
page 116. Instructions
    for making it on page
    114.

Constructing the cake

Scale up and cut out the template. Place on the cake and cut out the koala shape and the extension of the branch. Transfer the internal design lines to be iced in dark brown with a cocktail stick, skewer or sharp knife. Lift the two pieces of cake on to the cake board. Join the pieces of branch together with a little butter icing.

Icing the cake

Divide the butter icing into 3 bowls and colour: 3 tablespoons green flecked with a little cocoa powder, 2 tablespoons dark brown, 10 tablespoons honey brown. Don't mix the colours too well for this cake; an uneven colour will be more efective.

Roughly flat ice the branch with the green. Put a little of the dark brown icing on to a palette knife and mix lightly into the green to represent knots in the branch. Put the dark brown icing into an icing bag fitted with a thick writer tube and pipe on the pricked outlines of the bear. Fill a clean bag fitted with the star tube with honey brown icing and rosette the remainder of the cake including the paw on the branch. With a skewer or fork, go over the honey brown and lift it to give the effect of fur, especially around the ears. Work a little of the dark brown into the honey brown around the ears to give them depth.

Decorating the cake

Keep back ½ teaspoon of the fondant and colour the remainder black. Roll and cut out the nose and eyes using the template. Make up the eyes and nose with the white and black fondant and position on the cake. Roll the black in the palms of your hands to form claws, 10 will be needed. Take a teaspoonful of the honey brown butter icing and colour it black. Place the icing directly in the fine writer tube, and by exerting pressure with your thumb, pipe on the mouth and eyebrows.

KOALA BEAR

THE BUTTERFLY

Timing
2 hours to ice and
    decorate

Equipment
4 bowls for icing mixture
4 icing bags
2 tubes: star, medium
    writer
palette knife
cocktail stick or skewer
sharp knife
tracing paper
13 in cake board

Ingredients
1 cake, 8×12 in (page
    11), cooled upside
    down
1 quantity of butter icing
    (page 12)
food colouring: black,
    rose pink, violet, sky
    blue
apricot glaze (optional –
    page 12)

Template
page 117. Instructions
    for making it on page
    114.

Decoration
fuse wire

Constructing the cake

Scale up and cut out the template. Place on the cake and cut around the butterfly shape. Prick out the shape of the body with a cocktail stick, skewer or sharp knife. Lift the cake on to the board.

Icing the cake

Divide the butter icing into 4 bowls and colour: 2 tablespoons black, 5½ tablespoons rose pink, 2 tablespoons violet, 5½ tablespoons sky blue.

Using the photograph as a guide, roughly flat ice the pink area on either side of the body. With the sky blue and a clean palette knife, roughly flat ice out to the sides, merging the blue and the pink together. With the knife, make some wavy lines down the wings to provide texture. Flat ice the sides of the head and tail with the black. Put the remaining black in an icing bag fitted with the star tube and rosette in the body.

With a cocktail stick mark out where the violet edging and the design lines on the wings are to go using the template or the photograph as a guide. In a clean bag fitted with the star tube and violet icing, rosette the edging. Change the tube to a medium writer and pipe in the circles on the wings; 2 on either side at the top and one either side of the tail. Dot in 2 small eyes on the head and pipe the design lines on the wings.

Put the rest of the pink icing in a clean bag fitted with a star tube and rosette the top outer side of each wing. Rosette four small stars into the violet circles on the wings. With a clean bag, the star tube and sky blue, rosette the remaining sides of the butterfly.

Decoration

Cut two equal lengths of fuse wire, 6 in long, wrap them around a thin pencil and pull off. This gives coils for the antenna. Insert them into the head.

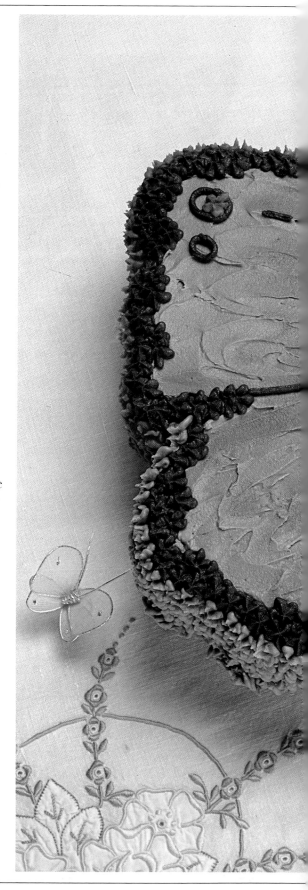

THE BUTTERFLY

Timing
2 hours to ice and
    decorate

Equipment
4 bowls for icing mixture
4 icing bags
2 tubes: star, medium
    writer
palette knife
cocktail stick or skewer
sharp knife
tracing paper
13 in cake board

Ingredients
1 cake, 8×12 in (page
    11), cooled upside
    down
1 quantity of butter icing
    (page 12)
food colouring: black,
    rose pink, violet, sky
    blue
apricot glaze (optional –
    page 12)

Template
page 117. Instructions
    for making it on page
    114.

Decoration
fuse wire

Constructing the cake
Scale up and cut out the template. Place on
the cake and cut around the butterfly shape.
Prick out the shape of the body with a
cocktail stick, skewer or sharp knife. Lift the
cake on to the board.

Icing the cake
Divide the butter icing into 4 bowls and
colour: 2 tablespoons black, 5½
tablespoons rose pink, 2 tablespoons violet,
5½ tablespoons sky blue.

Using the photograph as a guide, roughly
flat ice the pink area on either side of the
body. With the sky blue and a clean palette
knife, roughly flat ice out to the sides,
merging the blue and the pink together.
With the knife, make some wavy lines down
the wings to provide texture. Flat ice the
sides of the head and tail with the black. Put
the remaining black in an icing bag fitted
with the star tube and rosette in the body.

With a cocktail stick mark out where the
violet edging and the design lines on the
wings are to go using the template or the
photograph as a guide. In a clean bag fitted
with the star tube and violet icing, rosette the
edging. Change the tube to a medium writer
and pipe in the circles on the wings; 2 on
either side at the top and one either side of
the tail. Dot in 2 small eyes on the head and
pipe the design lines on the wings.

Put the rest of the pink icing in a clean bag
fitted with a star tube and rosette the top
outer side of each wing. Rosette four small
stars into the violet circles on the wings.
With a clean bag, the star tube and sky blue,
rosette the remaining sides of the butterfly.

Decoration
Cut two equal lengths of fuse wire, 6 in
long, wrap them around a thin pencil and
pull off. This gives coils for the antenna.
Insert them into the head.

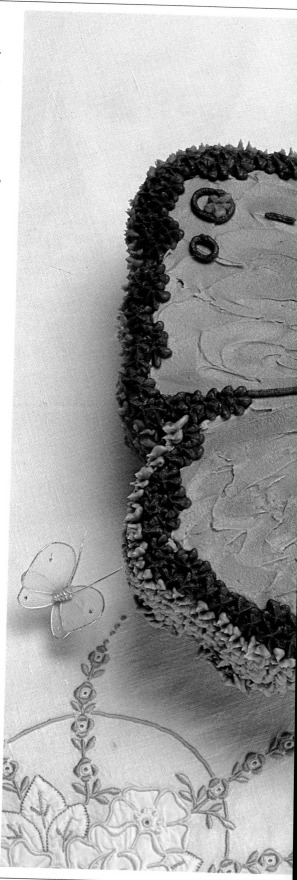

HORSE'S HEAD

KOALA BEAR

Timing
2 hours to ice and
    decorate

Equipment
3 bowls for icing mixture
2 icing bags
3 tubes: star, thick
    writer, fine writer
palette knife
sharp knife
fork
cocktail stick or skewer
tracing paper
13 in cake board

Ingredients
1 cake, 8×12 in (page
    11), cooled upside
    down
1 quantity of butter icing
    (page 12)
2 tablespoons fondant
    (page 16)
food colouring: grass
    green, black, honey
    brown (cocoa powder
    with a little yellow),
    cocoa powder
apricot glaze (optional –
    page 12)

Template
page 116. Instructions
    for making it on page
    114.

Constructing the cake

Scale up and cut out the template. Place on
the cake and cut out the koala shape and the
extension of the branch. Transfer the
internal design lines to be iced in dark brown
with a cocktail stick, skewer or sharp knife.
Lift the two pieces of cake on to the cake
board. Join the pieces of branch together
with a little butter icing.

Icing the cake

Divide the butter icing into 3 bowls and
colour: 3 tablespoons green flecked with a
little cocoa powder, 2 tablespoons dark
brown, 10 tablespoons honey brown. Don't
mix the colours too well for this cake; an
uneven colour will be more efective.

Roughly flat ice the branch with the green.
Put a little of the dark brown icing on to a
palette knife and mix lightly into the green to
represent knots in the branch. Put the dark
brown icing into an icing bag fitted with a
thick writer tube and pipe on the pricked
outlines of the bear. Fill a clean bag fitted
with the star tube with honey brown icing
and rosette the remainder of the cake
including the paw on the branch. With a
skewer or fork, go over the honey brown and
lift it to give the effect of fur, especially
around the ears. Work a little of the dark
brown into the honey brown around the ears
to give them depth.

Decorating the cake

Keep back 1/2 teaspoon of the fondant and
colour the remainder black. Roll and cut out
the nose and eyes using the template. Make
up the eyes and nose with the white and
black fondant and position on the cake. Roll
the black in the palms of your hands to form
claws, 10 will be needed. Take a teaspoonful
of the honey brown butter icing and colour it
black. Place the icing directly in the fine
writer tube, and by exerting pressure with
your thumb, pipe on the mouth and
eyebrows.

THE CAT

Timing
1½-2 hours to ice and
    decorate

Equipment
3 bowls for icing mixture
2 icing bags
3 tubes: star, medium
    and fine writer
palette knife
cocktail stick or skewer
sharp knife
tracing paper
13 in cake board

Ingredients
1 cake, 8×12 in (page
    11), cooled upside
    down
1 quantity of white
    butter icing (page 13)
1 tablespoon fondant
    (page 16)
food colouring: black,
    yellow
apricot glaze (optional –
    page 12)

Template
page 116. Instructions
    for making it on page
    114.

Constructing the cake

Scale up and cut out the template. Place on the cake and cut out the cat shape. Prick through the internal design lines, except the whiskers and the eyes. Lift the cake on to the board.

Icing the cake

Divide the butter icing into 3 bowls and colour: 2 tablespoons black, 2 tablespoons white, 11 tablespoons grey. With black, flat ice the tail, smoothing out to the sides. put the remaining black into an icing bag fitted with a medium writer tube and pipe on the pricked outlines for the body, face and paws. Put the black in the icing bag to one side for the moment. Fill a clean bag with white icing and using a star tube rosette on the white markings on the face and chest bag, the star tube and the grey, rosette the remainder of the cake.

Decorating the cake

Colour half the fondant black and the other half yellow. Roll out both the yellow and black fondant. Make the nose from the black and position on the cake. Cut out the eyes from the yellow. Using the black butter icing in the bag, pipe on the mouth and the pupils in the eyes. Change the tube on the white icing bag to a fine writer and pipe on the whiskers using the template or the photograph as a guide.

We have decorated with chocolate mice but the cat could have a ribbon around its neck – though don't attach this until just before the cake is to be served.

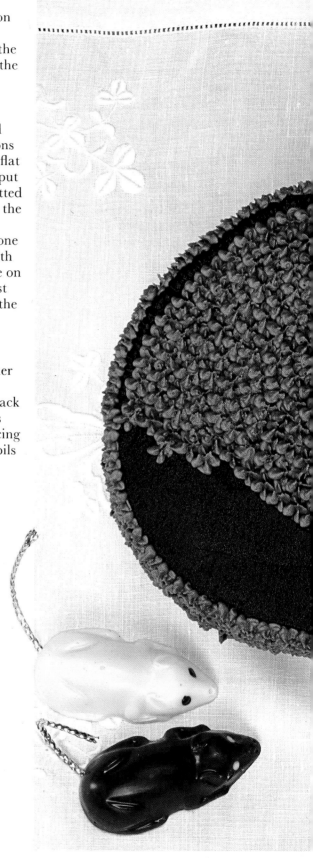

THE CAT

THREE RABBITS IN BED

THREE RABBITS IN BED

Timing
3-4 hours to ice and
  decorate

Equipment
2 bowls for icing mixture
2 icing bags
2 tubes: star, medium
  writer
palette knife
sharp knife
cocktail stick or skewer
tracing paper
heart-shaped cutters
paint brush
13 in cake board

Ingredients
1 cake, 8×12 in (page
  11), cooled upside
  down
1 quantity of white
  butter icing (page 13)
1 lb fondant (page 16)
food colouring: orange,
  yellow, choose your
  own colours for the
  bedspread, 4-5 will
  do, black, Christmas
  red
apricot glaze (optional –
  page 12)

Template
page 116. Instructions
  for making it on page
  114.

Decoration
tiny book
sugar-covered buttons
china miniatures
postcards of children's
  favourite storybook
  characters

Constructing the cake
Scale up and cut out the template. Place
on the cake and cut out the shapes. Lift the
bed shape (C) on to the cake board.

Icing the cake
Divide the butter icing into 2 bowls and
colour: 5 tablespoons white, 10 tablespoons
orange. With white icing flat ice the sides
and top of the bed, smoothing neatly
across the pillow area. Save a little white
for the designs on the head and base
boards. With orange icing and a clean
palette knife, flat ice the inside.f the head
(A) and base boards (B). Place them at
either end of the bed. The butter icing will
hold them in place. Flat ice the outside of
the boards.

Decorating the cake
Take a piece of the fondant and roll it out.
Cut into 3 pillows to fit across the bed.
Prick out the stitching lines on the pillows
with a cocktail stick and with a paint brush
and yellow food colouring, paint in the tiny
flowers. Place on the bed. Roll 3 small
pieces of fondant to represent the bodies
and place them on the bed below each
pillow.

Colour 3 tablespoons of fondant with a
little black to make a grey colour. Roll out
in your hands three round pieces for the
head (**1**), and 6 longer pieces for the ears
(**2**). Make indentations inside the ears with
your little finger (**3**).

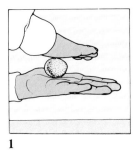
1

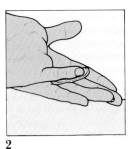
2

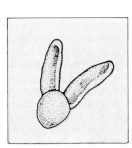
3

THREE RABBITS IN BED

With a clean paint brush, paint on the eyes and whiskers with black paint and the nose and inside the ears with red. Put the ears on the pillows and press the heads on to them. Measure from the chins to the base of the bed, and across the bed and down both sides. roll out the remainder of the fondant and cut a piece to these dimensions for the bedspread. Cut another piece of fondant for the turnback: the width of the bed plus overhang and about 1 in wide. Carefully drape the bedspread over the rabbits, making sure it extends to the cake board on either side. Place the turnback on top beneath the rabbits' chins. Prick the stitching lines with a cocktail stick. With a clean paint brush, paint the turnback to match the pillows.

Choose the colours you want for the bedspread. Dip the brush into the food colouring and paint directly on to the cover, cleaning your brush in water before changing colours. Here we have a random patchwork but you might like to do a pretty floral or a bright stripe.

Roll out the off cuts of fondant and cut out 6 tiny hearts with cutters or by hand. Place them firmly against the bed headboard and base. Add the decorations. We have made a tiny paper book, but this could easily be made out of fondant. Those with a steady hand could write in the title with food colouring. With any left-over fondant, you could make tiny slippers for the rabbits and place them at the foot of the bed.

Additional hints
This idea could be adapted to many fairy tales; for example, Sleeping Beauty, Red Riding Hood, Goldilocks. It could also be adapted to a get-well-soon cake. Sleeping Beauty could have glorious long strands of hair piped with butter icing on the bedspread. You could make a splendid bedspread by piping lines with butter icing onto the fondant in a pattern to suggest a rich brocade.

Fondant is so easy to shape and if you felt really adventurous, you could make the bedspread with a frilled skirt. Roll out a strip of fondant and pleat, then press against the side of the bed.

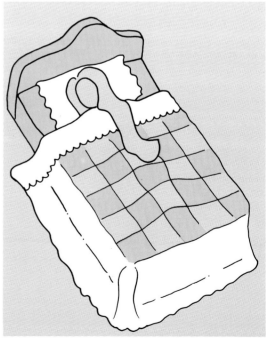

THE RABBIT

Timing
2 hours to ice and
    decorate

Equipment
2 bowls for icing mixture
2 icing bags
2 tubes: star, medium
    writer
palette knife
sharp knife
cocktail stick or skewer
tracing paper
13 in cake board

Ingredients
1 cake, 8×12 in (page
    11), cooled upside
    down
1 quantity of white
    butter icing (page 13)
    food colouring: rose
    pink

Template
page 117. Instructions for
    making it on page 114.

Constructing the cake
Scale up and cut out the template. Place it on
the cake and cut out the rabbit shape.
Transfer the internal design lines on to the
cake shape with a cocktail stick, skewer or
sharp knife. Lift the cake on to the board.

Icing the cake
Divide the butter icing into 2 bowls and
colour: 13 tablespoons white, 2 tablespoons
pink. Fill an icing bag fitted with the star
tube with the pink icing and rosette in the
ear and tail. Change the nozzle to the
medium writer and pipe a dot for the eye
and nose. Smooth these dots with a wet
palette knife. Pipe in the line for the leg.
Put the pink icing bag to one side for a
moment. Fill a clean icing bag, fitted with
the star tube, with the white icing and
rosette the rest of the cake using the leg
line as a guide.

When you reach the eye and nose, rosette
close to the finished shape as shown on your

template. With the pink icing bag finish off
the cake by piping the outline of the eyes and
nose and pipe in the whiskers and the mouth
using the template or photograph as a guide.

Additional hint
A bunch of fresh or artificial daffodils placed
close to the rabbit's paws would give a
springtime feel to this cake.

41

FREDDIE FROG

Timing
2 hours to ice and
decorate

Equipment
4 bowls for icing mixture
4 icing bags
2 tubes: star, medium
writer
palette knife
sharp knife
cocktail stick or skewer
tracing paper
13 in cake board

Ingredients
1 cake, 8×12 in (page
11), cooled upside
down
1 quantity of white
butter icing (page 13)
2 tablespoons fondant
(page 16)
food colouring:
Christmas red, yellow,
grass green, lime
green (grass green and
yellow), black
apricot glaze (optional –
page 12)

Template
page 117. Instructions
for making it on page
114.

Constructing the cake
Scale up and cut out the template. Place on
the cake and cut out the frog shape. Prick
through the eye and bowtie design lines with
a cocktail stick, skewer or sharp knife. Lift
the cake on to the board.

Icing the cake
Divide the butter icing into 4 bowls and
colour: 11 tablespoons green, 2 tablespoons
yellow, 1 tablespoon white, 1 tablespoon
lime green. With the green icing, flat ice
the top of the cake leaving out the eye and
bowtie area. Smooth out to the sides. Put
the white icing into a bag fitted with a star
tube and rosette the eyes and two rows of
stars around where the tongue will be. Fill
a clean bag with the yellow and the star
tube and rosette the bowtie. With another
clean bag, the star tube and green, rosette
the sides of the cake. Fit the medium writer
tube to a clean bag and with the lime
green, pipe the outlines around the frog,
piping in the arm and hand using the
template or the photograph as a guide.
You may find the arm and hand easier if
you lightly prick out the shape beforehand.

Decorating the cake
Colour a teaspoonful of the fondant black
and the remainder red. Make two small dots
for the eyes and two small crescents from the
black (see photograph). Place on the cake.
Roll out the red fondant and cut out a shape
for the tongue using the template. With the
base of a tube press out the dots for the
bowtie. Put the tongue in place and the dots
on the tie.

We made a lily leaf from a piece of felt; paper
would do as well, though it must be grease-
resistant. Add any pond-loving insects and
paper flowers.

FREDDIE FROG

THE BUTTERFLY

Timing
2 hours to ice and
  decorate

Equipment
4 bowls for icing mixture
4 icing bags
2 tubes: star, medium
  writer
palette knife
cocktail stick or skewer
sharp knife
tracing paper
13 in cake board

Ingredients
1 cake, 8×12 in (page
  11), cooled upside
  down
1 quantity of butter icing
  (page 12)
food colouring: black,
  rose pink, violet, sky
  blue
apricot glaze (optional –
  page 12)

Template
page 117. Instructions
  for making it on page
  114.

Decoration
fuse wire

Constructing the cake
Scale up and cut out the template. Place on
the cake and cut around the butterfly shape.
Prick out the shape of the body with a
cocktail stick, skewer or sharp knife. Lift the
cake on to the board.

Icing the cake
Divide the butter icing into 4 bowls and
colour: 2 tablespoons black, 5½
tablespoons rose pink, 2 tablespoons violet,
5½ tablespoons sky blue.

Using the photograph as a guide, roughly
flat ice the pink area on either side of the
body. With the sky blue and a clean palette
knife, roughly flat ice out to the sides,
merging the blue and the pink together.
With the knife, make some wavy lines down
the wings to provide texture. Flat ice the
sides of the head and tail with the black. Put
the remaining black in an icing bag fitted
with the star tube and rosette in the body.

With a cocktail stick mark out where the
violet edging and the design lines on the
wings are to go using the template or the
photograph as a guide. In a clean bag fitted
with the star tube and violet icing, rosette the
edging. Change the tube to a medium writer
and pipe in the circles on the wings; 2 on
either side at the top and one either side of
the tail. Dot in 2 small eyes on the head and
pipe the design lines on the wings.

Put the rest of the pink icing in a clean bag
fitted with a star tube and rosette the top
outer side of each wing. Rosette four small
stars into the violet circles on the wings.
With a clean bag, the star tube and sky blue,
rosette the remaining sides of the butterfly.

Decoration
Cut two equal lengths of fuse wire, 6 in
long, wrap them around a thin pencil and
pull off. This gives coils for the antenna.
Insert them into the head.

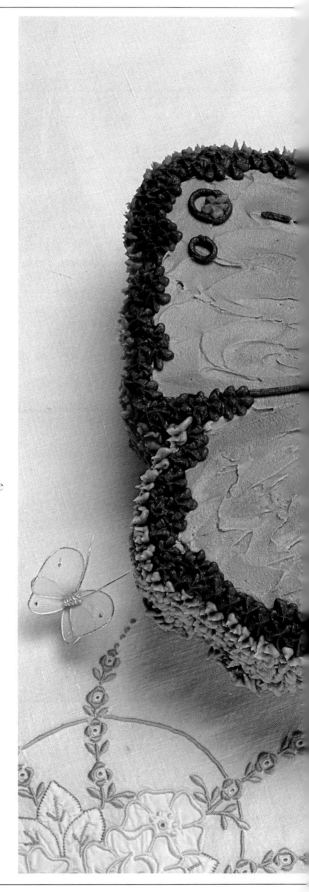

RACING CAR

Timing
3-4 hours to ice and
decorate

Equipment
4 bowls for icing mixture
4 icing bags
3 tubes: star, ribbing,
thick writer
palette knife
cocktail stick
tracing paper
13 in cake board

Ingredients
1 cake, 8×12 in (page
11), cooled upside
down
1 quantity of white
butter icing (page 13)
3 tablespoons fondant
(page 16)
food colouring:
Christmas red, royal
blue, cocoa powder
apricot glaze (optional –
page 12)

Template
page 117. Instructions
for making it on page
114.

Decoration
ice cream wafers
cocktail stick

Constructing the cake

Scale up and cut out the template. Place on the cake and cut out the 10 pieces of the racing car. Keep the tracing paper and the identifying letter with each piece so that you will be able to keep track of the pieces.

Shape the front of A down at an angle. Slice E and F in half crosswise and place them on the board. These form a platform to raise the body of the car. Slice diagonally through B to form 2 triangular pieces B1 and B2 (**1**). Slice C diagonally but slightly off centre to form C1 and C2 (**2**). Slice through D diagonally to make D1, discard the other triangular section (**3**). Following the assembly plan (**4**), join the pieces together with a little butter icing: place A on top of E and F, then position B1 and B2 at the back, and D1, C1 and C2 at the front. Leave the seat space between the two.

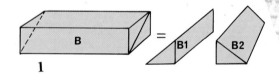

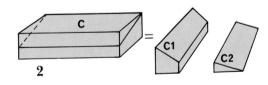

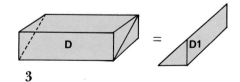

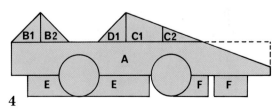

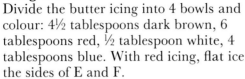

RACING CAR

Icing the cake

Divide the butter icing into 4 bowls and colour: 4½ tablespoons dark brown, 6 tablespoons red, ½ tablespoon white, 4 tablespoons blue. With red icing, flat ice the sides of E and F.

Using the picture as a guide to colours, flat ice the seat and doors with blue. Flat ice the back and sloping front with red. Take care where the two colours meet that they do not

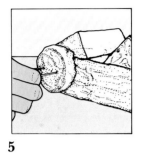

5

smudge together. Put the red icing in an icing bag fitted with a star tube and rosette around the sides of the car. Cut the ice cream wafers to the width of the car for the front and back and one wafer slightly narrower for the windscreen. Make a small incision with a sharp knife and insert the wafers in place. Put the rest of the blue into a clean bag fitted with the ribbing tube and pipe the line down the front and back of the car, across the base of the windscreen, down the sides of the seating compartment, around the doors and across the back and front. This gives a neat finish where the blue and red meet. With the white icing and the ribbing tube, pipe a white line down the front and back of the car next to the blue.

Wheels

Using dark brown, flat ice the outside of the tyres, smoothing with a wet palette knife. Place them on the cake; the best way to do this is to insert two cocktail sticks into the wheel and pick it up with the sticks (**5**). Try not to touch the flat iced sections. If you do, smooth again with a wet palette knife. The icing will hold the wheels against the cake. Put the rest of the dark brown into a bag fitted with a thick writer tube and pipe circles around the wheels to give a spiral effect. Make occasional indentations in the rims of the wheels with a cocktail stick to represent the tyre tread.

Decorating the cake

Colour 2 tablespoons of the fondant blue and the rest red.

Roll out and from the blue cut the windscreen wipers, the seats, door handles, safety belts, dashboard and back bumper and part of the design on the bonnet; use the photograph as a guide. From the red cut the headlamps, brake lights, belt clasps, bonnet design and any detail you want on the dashboard. All of these items can be adapted to your own design. The child's age, for example, could be the design on the bonnet.

Steering wheel

Cut a small circle out of a wafer and push a cocktail stick through it. Place a tiny piece of fondant on the tip of the cocktail stick for the horn. Insert the wheel into the cake.

RACING TRACK, No. 8

Timing
1-2 hours to ice and
  decorate

Equipment
3 bowls for icing mixture
1 icing bag
2 tubes: star, fine writer
sharp knife
palette knife
tracing paper
cocktail stick or skewer
paint brush
13 in cake board

Ingredients
1 cake, 8×12 in (page
  11), cooled upside
  down
1 quantity of butter icing
  page 12)
food colouring: green,
  black
apricot glaze (optional –
  page 12)

Template
page 118. Instructions
  for making it on page
  114.

Decoration

Numbers
On page 118 you will
  find templates for the
  other numbers. They
  can all be sut from a
  8×12 in cake (page
  11). They can, of
  course, be iced plain
  or, like the number 8,
  be turned into
  something special.

Constructing the cake
Scale up and cut out the template. Place on
the cake and cut around the number eight.
Prick through the centre outlines with a
cocktail stick, skewer or sharp knife. Lift the
cake on to the board.

Icing the cake
Divide the butter icing into 3 bowls and
colour: 1 tablespoon white, 7 tablespoons
grey, 7 tablespoons green. With the grey,
flat ice the track area on the cake. Don't
smooth to the edge. Leave about ¼ in
around the outer edge of the cake for a row
of green rosettes. In the centre, one track
should overlap the other, so build it up to

give a bridge effect. Put the green icing in a
bag fitted with the star tube and rosette the
two centre pieces and the sides of the cake.
With the white icing, in a clean bag fitted
with the fine writer tube, draw in the start
and finish lines. If you want skid marks,
dip the paint brush in black food colouring
and lightly brush around the curves.

Decoration
Make a chequered flag and join a piece of
paper to two cocktail sticks for the finish line.
Cut two sandwich flags into triangles and
insert into the cake. If you want to, you can
position cars on the track.

CANOE

Timing
2½-3 hours to ice and
decorate

Equipment
2 bowls for icing mixture
1 icing bag
1 tube: ribbing
palette knife
sharp knife
cocktail stick or skewer
tracing paper
13 in cake board

Ingredients
1 cake, 8×12 in (page
11), cooled upside
down
1 quantity of butter icing
(page 12)
5 tablespoons fondant
(page 16)
food colouring: black,
sky blue, Christmas
red, cocoa powder,
Indian brown (cocoa
powder and orange)
apricot glaze (optional –
page 12)

Template
page 119. Instructions for
making it on page 114.
The template for the
base will need to be
scaled up but the
fondant shapes are the
actual size needed for
this cake. Simply trace
them from the book.

Constructing the cake

Scale up and cut out the template for the
base. Cut the cake in half lengthwise and lift
one half on to the board. Place the other half
on top of it, joining together with a little
butter icing.

Place the template on the 2 cakes and cut
around the shape. Hollow out the canoe to
half the depth of the top piece of cake,
curving the sides as well. Make two points at
either end of the canoe with the offcuts,
joined on with butter icing (see below).

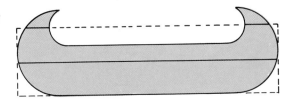

Icing the cake

Divide the butter icing into 2 bowls and
colour: 13 tablespoons Indian brown, 2
tablespoons brown. Roughly flat ice the
cake in the Indian brown, moving the wet
palette knife along the sides and up to the
points. Put the dark brown into an icing
bag fitted with the ribbing tube and pipe
lengthwise along the floor of the canoe.
Pipe three double lines across the canoe for
seats. Then pipe the paddles on each side.

Decorating the cake

Roll out the fondant and using the templates,
cut out the shapes. Prick out the designs with
a pin. With a paint brush and food colouring,
paint on your designs, using the photograph
as reference for the colour combinations.
Place them on to the canoe before they are
dry so that they will curve to fit it.

Additional hints

The paddles could be made out of wooden
lollipop sticks cut to shape. The cake could
be adapted to other types of boat, such as a
gondola. It could be filled with sugar, paper
or fondant flowers (page 17).
    You could make a rowing boat by laying
the two lengths end to end, filling the hollow
with fondant rowers and making oars from
cocktail sticks.

CANOE

TRAIN

Timing
3 hours to ice and decorate

Equipment
5 bowls for icing mixture
4 icing bags
2 tubes: star, ribbing
palette knife
sharp knife
cocktail stick or skewer
tracing paper
15 in cake board

Ingredients
2 cakes, 8×12 in (page 11), cooled upside down
2 quantities of butter icing (page 12)
4 tablespoons fondant (page 16)
food colouring: Christmas red, lemon yellow, sky blue, egg yellow, violet, black
apricot glaze (optional – page 12)

Template
page 120. Instructions for making it on page 114.

Constructing the cake
Scale up and cut out the templaes. Place on the cakes and cut out the 10 pieces. Keep the tracing paper on the pieces so that you can identify them. Slice J in half crosswise to make J1 and J2. Using the plan below as a guide (**1**) assemble the cake on the board, using about 2 tablespoons of the butter icing to join the pieces. Start with the base A, then make up the next two layers with B, C, D and E. Raise the cabin at the rear with F, G and J1. With a sharp knife, shape the sides of the top two pieces at the front of the train to form the engine (**2**). Curve out the back of the train cabin. Make up the coal truck on the cake board just behind the train with H, I and then J2. Cut out a curve at the front.

Icing the cake
Divide the butter icing into 5 bowls and colour: 6 tablespoons red, 8 tablespoons lemon yellow, 4 tablespoons egg yellow, 6 tablespoons violet, 4 tablespoons sky blue. With the lemon yellow, flat ice the engine, the curve of the cabin and the curve of the coal truck. Put the egg yellow in an icing bag fitted with a ribbing tube and pipe in the yellow lines over the engine and around the cabin and coal truck. Rosette the top of the coal truck. Put the bag of egg yellow to one side.

Put the red icing into a bag fitted with a star tube and rosette the cabin, the front of the engine, the front of the coal truck and around its shape. Rosette the rest of the train.

Decorating the cake
Colour half the fondant violet and the other half black. From the black, shape 6 wheels and a funnel. As the funnel will need support, colour the tip of a long cocktail stick black and insert it through the funnel and into the cake. Chop up the remaining black fondant into pieces to look like coal. Put on to the shelf on the coal truck. From the violet fondant shape 3 pieces for the top of the train engine (see photograph), 2 windows, 6 wheels and the front grill on the engine. Position all the fondant pieces as shown. Pipe on to the wheels with the yellow icing.

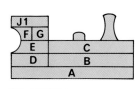

1

2

TANK

Timing
2-3 hours to ice and
 decorate

Equipment
3 bowls for icing mixture
2 icing bags
2 tubes: star, medium
 writer
palette knife
sharp knife
cocktail stick or skewer
tracing paper
13 in cake board

Ingredients
1 cake, 8×12 in (page
 11), cooled upside
 down
1 quantity of butter icing
 (page 12)
2½ tablespoons
 marzipan (page 16)
food colouring: army
 green (green and
 yellow), army yellow
 (cocoa and yellow),
 cocoa powder
apricot glaze (optional –
 page 12)

Template
page 119. Instructions for
 making it on page 114.

Decoration
toffee apple stick
plastic soldiers
sparkler
chocolate buttons

TANK

Constructing the cake

Scale up and cut out the template. Place on the cake and cut around the 6 shapes. Using the butter icing to join the pieces, place A on top of B to form the base. Join D and C to either side with the shorter section at the bottom. Place the cabin E to the back of the base section. Shape the hatch F at an angle and join to the top of the cabin at the back.

Icing the cake

Divide the butter icing into 3 bowls and colour: 6 tablespoons army green, 6 tablespoons army yellow, 3 tablespoons brown. With army green, flat ice the front and back of the tank tracks. Put the brown icing in a bag fitted with a star tube and rosette around the sides of the cabin and the hatch. Change to the medium writer tube and pipe in the track marks on the green flat-iced tracks. Change to a clean bag with the army green and rosette the green parts of the camouflage including the top of the cabin. Change to a clean bag and the yellow, and finish covering the cake with rosettes, including the top part of the hatch.

Decorating the cake

Place the chocolate buttons on the side of the tank using the photograph as a guide. Divide the marzipan in half and colour one half army green and the other army yellow. Now lightly blend them together to get a marbled effect for your camouflage. Roll out the marzipan and cover the toffee apple stick, leaving 3 in of the stick uncovered at one end. Make a hole with the skewer at the base of the cabin front and insert the marzipan barrel into it at an angle. Out of the remaining marzipan, cut out 4 hatch-shaped pieces and place them on the cake as in the photograph. Add the plastic soldiers.

For this cake you could use a lighted sparkler in the barrel. The board could be made into a battlefield, though you would need to put the cake on a 16 in cake board for that.

FORT

Timing
2½ hours to ice and
   decorate

Equipment
2 bowls for icing mixture
2 icing bags
1 tube: star
palette knife
sharp knife
tracing paper
13 in cake board

Ingredients
1 cake, 8×12 in (page
   11), cooled upside
   down
1 quantity of butter icing
   (page 12)
food colouring: cocoa
   powder
apricot glaze (optional –
   page 12)

Template
page 119. Instructions for
   making it on page 114.

Decoration
14 chocolate finger
   biscuits
4 American flags
chocolate strands
4 square flat mints

Constructing the cake
Scale up and cut out the template. Place it on
the cake and cut out the 6 shapes. Lift the
large section for the base on to the cake
board.

Icing the cake
Divide the butter icing into 2 bowls and
colour: 7½ tablespoons dark brown, 7½
tablespoons light brown. Flat ice the sides
of the cake with the dark brown,
smoothing up to the edges. Flat ice the top
with the light brown. Flat ice the sides of
the 4 towers in dark brown and the tops in
light brown. Using a fish slice or two wide-
bladed palette knives, carefully position
each tower at a corner of the base about ¼
in in from the edge. The remaining piece of
cake is the entrance to the fort. Flat ice the
sides light brown and the top dark brown.
Put the rest of the dark brown icing in a
bag fitted with the star tube and rosette
around the top of the base cake and
around the top of each tower and the
entrance. Change to a clean bag with the
light brown icing and the star tube and
rosette around the base f the cake and
rosette a small square n each of the towers
to surround the flags.

Decorating the cake
Cut 12 of the chocolate fingers down to fit the
depth of the cake plus towers. Push 4 into the
corners and 8 into the cake as shown in the
photograph. Make incisions in the cake with
a sharp knife and place the mints between
the towers as shown. Position flags, soldiers
and Indians. Sprinkle chocolate strands over
the cake.

Additional hint
This cake would look more spectacular if you
used 2 cakes to give it more height.

FORT

OLD WOMAN WHO LIVED IN A SHOE

Timing
3+ hours to ice and decorate

Equipment
6 bowls for icing mixture
6 icing bags
4 tubes: star, ribbing, medium and thin writers
palette knife
sharp serrated knife
tracing paper
13 in cake board

Ingredients
1 cake, 8×12 in (page 11), cooled upside down
1 quantity of butter icing (page 12)
food colouring: egg yellow, rose, grass green, cocoa powder
apricot glaze (optional – page 12)

Template
page 120. Instructions for making it on page 114.

Decoration
ice cream wafers
sugar-covered buttons
sugar mushrooms
flower pots and boxes
children

Constructing the cake
Scale up and cut out the template. Place on the cake and cut out the 2 shapes. Lift the shoe on to the cake board. With a sharp knife, shave the roof section to make a sloping roof, and join it to the shoe with a little butter icing.

Icing the cake
Divide the butter icing into 6 bowls and colour: 1 tablespoon white, ½ tablespoon grass green, ½ tablespoon rose, 2 tablespoons dark brown, 7 tablespoons light brown, 4 tablespoons egg yellow. Begin by flat icing the top of the shoe with the light brown icing. Smooth out to the sides. With a cocktail stick, prick out where the door, windows and window boxes will go, using the photograph as a guide. With the white, flat ice the top of the windows and the top half of the door. Put the light brown into a bag fitted with a star tube and rosette around the sides of the shoe, leaving out the sole and heel as pictured.

Cut the wafer biscuits into 3 windows, 1 flower trough, 3 flower pots and the 2 sections of the door following the shapes on the template. Position wafers on the shoe, wedging the top section of the door to stand ajar. With white icing in a clean bag fitted with a medium writer tube, pipe on the window and door markings using the photograph as a guide. Change to a clean bag with the dark brown and the star tube and rosette the sole and heel. Change to a medium writer tube and pipe around the door, windows and the stitching and laces on the shoe.

Roughly flat ice the roof with the yellow icing. Mark out the thatching with the serrated knife or a bread knife (**1**). Put the green icing into a bag fitted with the thin writer tube and pipe in the storks, stems and leaves on the flowers and the climbing rose. Put the pink icing into a clean bag with a ribbing tube, and pipe in the flowers. Surround the cake with your decorations.

1

INCREDIBLE HULK

Timing
2 hours to ice and
   decorate

Equipment
2 bowls for icing mixture
1 icing bag
2 tubes: star, medium
   writers
palette knife
cocktail stick or skewer
tracing paper
paint brush
sharp knife
13 in cake board

Ingredients
1 cake, 8×12 in (page
   11), cooled upside
   down
1 quantity of butter icing
   (page 12)
2 tablespoons marzipan
   (page 16)
(If you buy the yellow
   marzipan you needn't
   bother with the yellow
   colouring.)
food colouring: grass
   green, black, lemon
   yellow
apricot glaze (optional –
   page 12)

Template
page 120. Instructions for
   making it on page 114.

Constructing the cake
Scale up and cut out the template. Place on
the cake and cut around the Hulk's shape.
Prick out the hairline with a cocktail stick,
skewer or sharp knife. Lift the cake on to the
board.

Icing the cake
Divide the butter icing into 2 bowls and
colour: 14 tablespoons green, 1 tablespoon
black. Flat ice the top of the cake with the
green icing, smoothing up to the hairline.
Put the remaining green icing into a bag
fitted with a star tube and rosette the hair
and around the sides of the cake. With a
clean bag, the black icing and a medium
writer tube, pipe on the outline of

the face and shoulders using the template or
the photograph as a guide. You may find it
easier to prick out this line on the butter
icing first.

Decorating the cake
If you don't have yellow marzipan, colour
the marzipan with the yellow colouring. Roll
it out and using the template, cut out the
eyes, mouth and nostrils. Prick in the design
lines on the mouth and eyes and paint in the
black sections with a paint brush dipped in
black food colouring. Position the marzipan
shapes on the face.

SPIDERMAN

Timing
2 hours to ice and
  decorate

Equipment
2 bowls for icing mixture
2 icing bags
2 tubes: medium writers,
  star
palette knife
sharp knife
cocktail stick or skewer
tracing paper
paint brush
13 in cake board

Ingredients
1 cake, 8×12 in (page
  11), cooled upside
  down
1 quantity of butter icing
  (page 12)
3 tablespoons marzipan
  (page 16)
food colouring:
  Christmas red, cocoa
  powder, silver food
  paint
apricot glaze (optional –
  page 12)

Template
page 122. Instructions for
  making it on page 114.

Constructing the cake
Scale up and cut out the template. Place it on the cake and cut out the shape. Lift on to the board.

Icing the cake
Divide the butter icing into 2 bowls and colour: 2 tablespoons brown, 13 tablespoons red. Roll out the marzipan and using the template for the eyes, cut out 2 eyes and paint with silver food colouring. Leave to dry. Flat ice the top of the cake with red icing, smoothing out to the sides. Place the eyes on the cake halfway between the chin and the top of the head and about ½ in apart. Using the template as a guide, prick in the lines of the webbing with a cocktail stick or skewer. Put the brown icing in a bag fitted with a medium writer tube and begin the webbing, starting with the oblong shape between the eyes, then piping the straight lines out to the edges and crossing them with curves for the web effect. Pipe in the triangles at the sides of the eyes and pipe lines close together until the space is filled. Pipe dots on the silver eyes.

Change to a clean bag with the star tube and the red icing and rosette the sides of the cake to finish. Remove the eyes before cutting as the silver food paint is not edible.

Additional hint
Pipe a red spider's web on to the cake board.

SPACE STATION

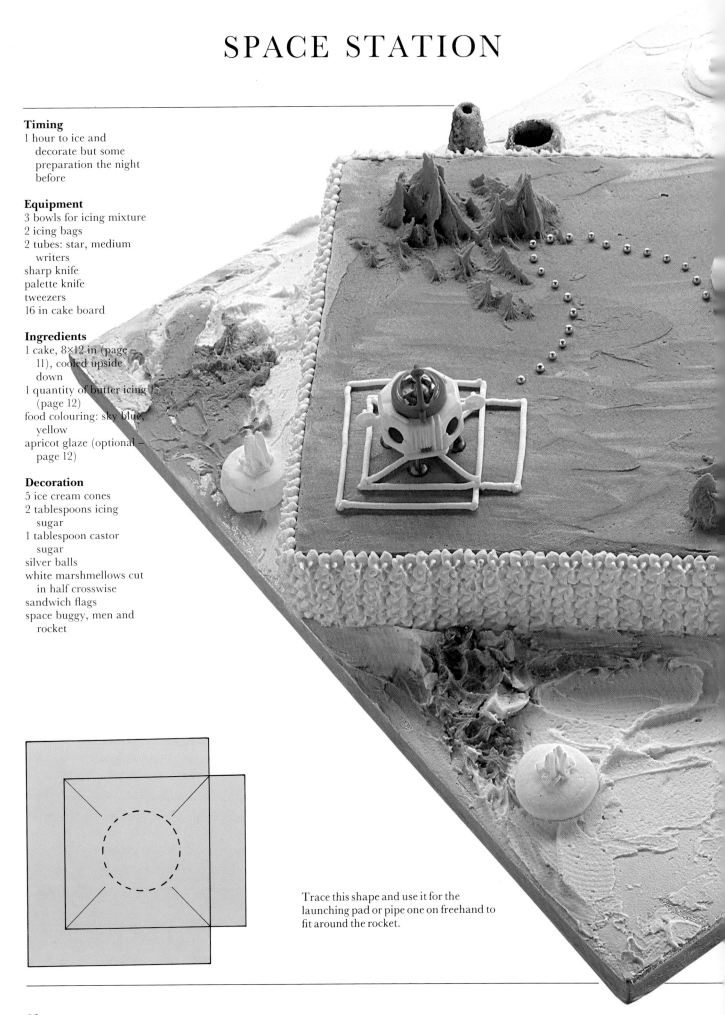

Timing
1 hour to ice and
decorate but some
preparation the night
before

Equipment
3 bowls for icing mixture
2 icing bags
2 tubes: star, medium
writers
sharp knife
palette knife
tweezers
16 in cake board

Ingredients
1 cake, 8×12 in (page
11), cooled upside
down
1 quantity of butter icing
(page 12)
food colouring: sky blue,
yellow
apricot glaze (optional –
page 12)

Decoration
5 ice cream cones
2 tablespoons icing
sugar
1 tablespoon castor
sugar
silver balls
white marshmellows cut
in half crosswise
sandwich flags
space buggy, men and
rocket

Trace this shape and use it for the
launching pad or pipe one on freehand to
fit around the rocket.

SPACE STATION

The night before
Make up a mixture of the icing sugar, castor sugar, sky blue colouring and enough water to make a thickish paste. Cut the ice cream cones into various sizes to represent the craters and peaks. Coat them with the blue paste and allow to dry on paper overnight. If they look washed out, recoat.

Icing the cake
Divide the butter icing into 3 bowls and colour: 7 tablespoons sky blue, 2 tablespoons white, 6 tablespoons yellow. Flat ice the top of the cake with sky blue, smoothing out to the edges. With a wet palette knife put some of the icing into a corner and peak by pressing down lightly and lifting. Repeat again on the opposite corner, varying the amount of icing to give large and small peaks.

Put the white icing into a bag fitted with the medium writer tube and pipe on the launching pad using the template below left. You can change this to fit the rocket. Change to a clean bag filled with the yellow and fitted with a star tube and rosette around the sides of the cake. Save some yellow icing for later.

Decorating the cake
Position the cones on the cake. Place the marshmallows, sticky side down, by the cones and pipe elongated yellow rosettes on top of each one. With a pair of tweezers, put the silver balls on to the cake to make a trail. Cut the sandwich flags to size and colour. We have extended the theme to the board.

WICKED WITCH

Timing
1½ hours to ice and
decorate

Equipment
5 bowls for icing mixture
2 icing bags
2 tubes: thick writer,
star
palette knife
sharp knife
cocktail stick or skewer
tracing paper
stainless steel cutters for
moon and star shapes
'? in cake board

Ingredients
1 cake, 8×8 in (page 11),
cooled upside down
1 quantity of butter icing
(page 12)
5 tablespoons marzipan
(page 16)
food colouring: lemon
yellow, violet, black,
sky blue
apricot glaze (optional –
page 12)

Constructing the cake
Trace the shape of the witch on paper and
cut out. Lift the cake on to the board.

Icing the cake
Divide the butter icing into 2 bowls and
colour: 2 tablespoons lemon yellow, 13
tablespoons violet. Flat ice the top of the
cake with the violet icing, smoothing out to
the sides. Put the remaining violet into a
bag fitted with the star tube and rosette the
sides.

Decorating the cake
Divide the marzipan into 3 bowls and
colour: 4 tablespoons black, ½ tablespoon
yellow, ½ tablespoon blue. Roll out the
black and lay the template for the witch on
to it. Cut out the witch. Roll out the yellow
and clue and using stainless steel cutters,
cut out 4 yellow stars and 2 blue stars and
one small blue moon. Use your discretion
as to the number of stars and what colours
they will be. You can make extra stars to
put around the cake and use as candle
holders. Carefully position the witch on the
cake. Put the yellow icing into a bag fitted
with the thick writer tube and pipe a semi-
circle from the brim of the witch's hat at
the back down to the cat's ears for the
outline of the moon. You may like to prick
this line out first before putting the icing
on the cake. Fill in the moon with ever-
decreasing circles; try not to make then too
even. Carefully position the stars on the
cake.

Additional hints
This cake could be used for Hallowe'en and
so a pumpkin, a haunted house, a cat or a bat
would be equally effective in the black
marzipan.

LADY ROBOT

Timing
2 hours to ice and
    decorate

Equipment
4 bowls for icing mixture
3 icing bags
2 tubes: star, medium
    writer
stainless steel cutters for
    star and spangle
    shapes
cocktail stick or skewer
sharp knife
tracing paper
paint brush
13 in cake board

Ingredients
1 cake, 8×12 in (page
    11), cooled upside
    down
1 quantity of butter icing
    (page 12)
3 tablespoons fondant
    (page 16)
food colouring: lemon
    yellow, sky blue, royal
    blue, silver food paint,
    Christmas red
apricot glaze (optional –
    page 12)

Template
page 122. Instructions for
    making it on page 114.

Decoration
fuse wire
silver balls

Constructing the cake
Scale up and cut out the template. Place on the cake and cut around the shape. Prick out the design lines using a cocktail stick, skewer or a sharp knife. Lift the cake on to the board.

Icing the cake
Divide the butter icing into 3 bowls and colour: 6 tablespoons yellow, 5 tablespoons, royal blue, 4 tablespoons sky blue. Fill an icing bag with yellow and attach the star tube. Rosette in the arms and head (there are 4 arms). Change to a clean bag with the medium writer tube and royal blue icing and pipe three lines across the cake. These are the lines in the photograph that have the silver balls placed along them. Change the tube to the star and rosette in the darker blue areas in the photograph. Change to a clean bag, with the sky blue and the star tube, and finish icing the cake.

Decorating the cake
Colour red ½ tablespoon of the fondant. Roll out and with small stainless steel cutters cut out a star and 6 triangles. Roll out the rest of the white fondant and using the cutters cut out 3 triangles and one star. Using the base of a tube, cut out 9 circles. Finally, using the template or freehand, cut out the 2 large and 2 small armbands. Place the fondant pieces on the cake. With the silver food paint and a paint brush, paint the armbands and circles. As the silver food paint isn't edible, you may prefer to leave these plain or remove them before cutting the cake. Place silver balls along the piped dark blue lines and around the wrists.

Cut fuse wire into 3 lengths about 8 in long. Wrap each one around a thin pencil, then pull off. This will give a springy coil for the antenna. Insert them into the cake at the head.

Additional hints
You can make this cake look as weird as you wish. Try lime green, shocking pink and brilliant orange. Fruit pastilles or licorice all-sorts can substitute for the fondant.

CLOWN FACE

Timing
2½-3 hours to ice and
  decorate

Equipment
4 bowls for icing mixture
4 icing bags
3 tubes: star, medium
  writer, ribbing
palette knife
cocktail stick or skewer
sharp knife
tracing paper
13 in cake board

Ingredients
1 cake, 8×12 in (page
  11), cooled upside
  down
1 quantity of white
  butter icing (page 13)
2 tablespoons fondant or
  marzipan (page 16)
food colouring: grass
  green, Christmas red,
  lemon yellow, cocoa
  powder
apricot glaze (optional –
  page 12)

Template
page 122. Instructions for
  making it on page 114.

Decoration
bowtie

Constructing the cake
Scale up and cut out the template. Place on
the cake and cut out the clown's face and the
pompom on his hat. Prick through the
design lines with a cocktail stick, skewer or
sharp knife. Lift the cake on to the board and
join the pieces together with a little of the
butter icing.

Icing the cake
Divide the butter icing into 4 bowls and
colour: 3 tablespoons white, 4 tablespoons,
brown, 4 tablespoons green, 4 tablespoons
yellow. Flat ice the face with the white
icing, smoothing out to the sides. Put the
rest of the white into a bag fitted with a
star tube and rosette down the sides of the
ears. Put the brown icing in a clean bag
fitted with the star tube and rosette in the
hair. Change to the medium writer and
pipe in the eyes, eyebrows, ears and chin
(keep a little aside for the mouth line on
the fondant). With green icing and the star
tube, rosette the hat. Change to the ribbing
tube and pipe in the lines of green on the
collar. Put the yellow icing in a clean bag
fitted with the star tube and rosette the
pompom on the hat and the collar. Change
to the ribbing tube and pipe on the dots on
the hat and a line around the neck.

Decorating the cake
Colour the fondant or marzipan red and roll
out. Using the template cut out the mouth.
Cut out 2 buttons with the base of a tube for
the nose and pompom. Make 14 small balls
and place them around the neck as shown in
the photograph. Place the fondant on the
cake and pipe in the brown line on the
mouth. Finally, attach the bowtie.

CLOWN FACE

TREASURE ISLAND

Timing
2 hours to ice and
   decorate

Equipment
6 bowls for icing mixture
3 icing bags
3 tubes: thick, medium
   and fine writer
sharp knife
palette knife
tracing paper
paint brush
13 in cake board

Ingredients
1 cake, 8×12 in (page
   11), cooled upside
   down
1 quantity of white
   butter icing (page 13)
food colouring: grass
   green, jungle green
   (yellow and green),
   yellow, royal blue,
   cocoa powder
apricot glaze (optional –
   page 12)

Template
page 122. Instructions for
   making it on page 114.

Decoration
2 palm trees
1 chenille bird
chocolate coins
yellow sugar-covered
   buttons

Constructing the cake

Scale up and cut out the template. Place on the cake and cut around the island shape. Place the cake on the board.

Icing the cake

Divide the butter icing into 6 bowls and colour: 5 tablespoons grass green, 5 tablespoons, jungle green, 1 tablespoon yellow, 2 tablespoons royal blue, 1 tablespoon brown, 1 tablespoon white. Flat ice one half of the cake with the grass green and the other with the jungle green, smoothing out to the sides. Leave an area for the yellow quicksand as shown in the photograph. Reserve some of the jungle green icing. Flat ice the yellow quicksand. Using a palette knife dipped in warm water, smooth over the whole cake blending the colours together to give a mottled effect.

Make the mountain range with the blue icing. Put teaspoonsful of the icing on to the cake and 'lift' the icing with the palette knife to form peaks. Make the lower jungle green mountain range in the same way. Put the remainder of the royal blue icing in an icing bag fitted with a thick writer tube and pipe around the base of the cake to form waves. Do two rows to give the sea some depth.

Change to the medium writer tube and pipe in the river, using the photograph as a guide. Put the white icing in a clean bag fitted with the medium writer and pipe on the white tops to the waves and the tips of the blue mountains. Change to a clean bag, brown icing and the fine writer tube and pipe in the place names. Finally add your decorations.

Additional hint

You could bury some treasure in the cake before you ice it. Cut a 3 in square out of the centre of the cake, cutting right through to the board but retaining the top ½ in as a lid. Fill the hole with smal chocolate coins or other treasure, replace the lid so that it is flush with the top of the cake. The icing will cover the joins. Remember to mark the spot with an 'X' so you don't slice through the treasure.

COTTAGE GARDEN

Timing
1 hour to ice and
 decorate

Equipment
2 bowls for icing mixture
1 icing bag
1 tube: star
palette knife
sharp knife
thick paint brush
13 in cake board

Ingredients
1 round cake, 8 in in
 diameter, baked in 2
 sandwich tins or 1
 deep tin (page 11),
 cooled right side up
1 quantity of butter icing
 (page 12)
1 tablespoon marzipan
 (page 16)
food colouring: mint
 green, sky blue
apricot glaze (optional –
 page 12)

Decoration
trees
100s and 1000s
golden syrup
pretzels
sugar flowers
ice cream wafers
sugar mushrooms
sugar ladybirds

Constructing the cake
If you baked 2 cakes, join them with butter
icing. Your cake will have risen slightly so
carefully cut the curved area for the path.
it should be about 1 in wide. Do not cut too
deeply; the cut is just to provide a better
surface for the wafers. Cut out a shallow
shape for the pool. We have made a kidney
shape. Lift the cake on to the cake board.

Icing the cake
Colour the marzipan sky blue and roll out.
Cut out the pool shape and place it on the
cake. Mix the green food colouring into the
butter icing. Roughly flat ice the sides and
top of the cake leaving the path area free. Cut
the ice cream wafers to fit the path and put
them in place. Put the rest of the green icing
in a bag fitted with the star tube and rosette

the borders of the path and one side of the
kidney-shaped pool.

Decorating the cake
Brush the trees in golden syrup and roll them
in 100s and 1000s. Leave to settle. Cut down
the pretzels and insert them round the cake
to make a fence. Place the other decorations
on the cake.

Additional hints
This simple cake can be adapted to any
interesting theme. You could add tiny frogs,
a house, plants and flowers. Alternatively it
could be turned into a farmyard with tiny
animals, or a zoo. Chocolate finger biscuits
could be used as a picket fence in place of the
pretzels.

SNOWY SCENE

Timing
1 hour to ice and
    decorate

Equipment
3 bowls for icing mixture
palette knife
sharp knife
13 in cake board

Ingredients
1 round cake, 8 in in
    diameter, baked in 2
    sandwich tins or 1
    deep tin (page 11),
    cooled upside down
1 quantity of white
    butter icing (page 13)
food colouring: royal
    blue, sky blue
apricot glaze (optional –
    page 12)

Decoration
fir trees
plastic snow figures
silver balls
sandwich flag
sugar snowmen
penguin

Constructing the cake
Join the cakes together with butter icing if
you have baked them in 2 tins. With a sharp
knife, cut a small wedge out of the cake at the
front and join this with butter icing to the
back to create a mound. Lift on to the board.

Icing the cake
Divide the butter icing into 3 bowls and
colour: 2 tablespoons royal blue, 1
tablespoon sky blue, the remainder leave
white. Roughly flat ice the sides of the cake
with white icing. Clean the palette knife
and ice the sides of the ledge and the
mound with the sky blue icing. Continue
rough icing the rest of the cake with white.
Put a little of the 2 blue icings on to the
palette knife and place them in clumps
around the base of the cake. Wet the
palette knife and swirl the icing, merging

the 2 colours together to give the effect of
waves lapping against the side.

Decorating the cake
Colour the sandwich flag and insert it into
the mound. Position the trees, figures and
silver balls.

Additional hints
This cake could be the North or South Pole
with an igloo made out of marzipan or
fondant. Or for a skiing enthusiast, make a
skiing slope with trees and a lone skier.

FAIRY CASTLE

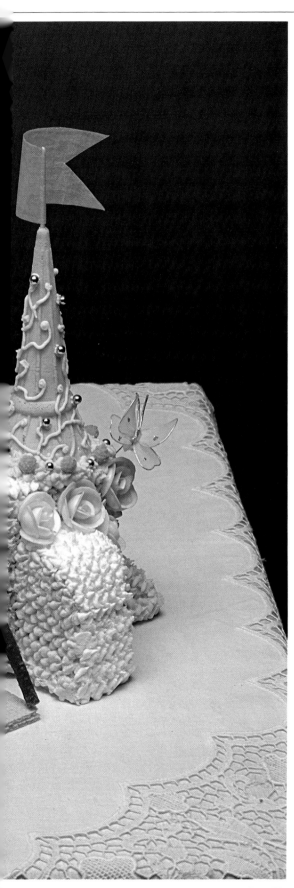

Timing
5 hours to ice and
   decorate

Equipment
4 bowls for icing mixture
4 icing bags
5 tubes: 4 stars, fine
   writer
palette knife
sharp knife
tracing paper
16 in cake board

Ingredients
2 cakes, 8×12 in (page
   11), cooled upside
   down
3 quantities of white
   butter icing (page 13)
food colouring: rose
   pink, lemon yellow
apricot glaze (optional –
   page 12)

Template
page 123. Instructions for
   making it on page 114.
   Read the instructions
   and study the plan (**1**)
   carefully.

Decoration
silver balls
sandwich flags
100s and 1000s
7 ice cream cones
2 packets of wafer biscuits
wafer roses
2 chocolate matchsticks
gauze butterflies

Constructing the cake
Scale up and cut out the templates. Place one
on each cake and cut out around all the
pieces, keeping the tracing with each piece
for identification. You should have 17 pieces.
Study the plan (**1**) before you begin. All the
pieces will be joined together with white
butter icing and covered with apricot glaze.

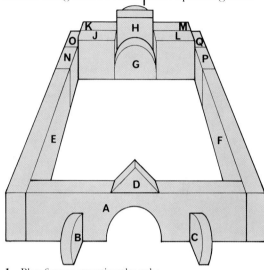

1. Plan for constructing the cake.

Icing the cake
Divide the butter icing into 4 bowls and
colour: 12 tablespoons white, 11
tablespoons dark rose pink, 11 tablespoons
pale rose pink, 11 tablespoons pale lemon
yellow. With white icing flat ice the inside
of the arch in A and place on the board.
Join B, C and D on to A. With a star tube
and pale yellow icing rosette one row
around the inside of wall A. Put the light
pink into a clean bag fitted with a star tube
and rosette a second row around the arch.
Put the dark pink in a bag fitted with a
star tube and rosette the rest of the inside
wall. Join E and N, F and P and lay

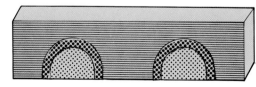

2. Colour scheme for inner sides.

them on their sides. Rosette their sides in the
illustrated colour scheme (**2**). Using a
palette knife and your hand, carefully lift the

FAIRY CASTLE

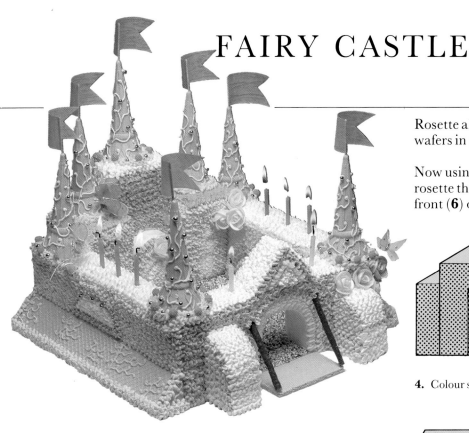

Rosette along the top, bottom and sides of the wafers in pale pink. This holds them in place.

Now using the illustrations as a colour guide, rosette the back (**4**), the sides (**5**), and the front (**6**) of the cake.

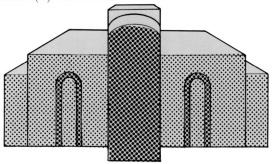

4. Colour scheme for outside back.

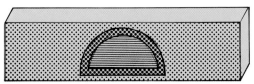

5. Colour scheme for outer sides.

sides and join them to the cake already on the board.

Flat ice the top of arch G with white icing. Join K, H and M. Join G to H and then J to K and L to M. Brush with apricot glaze. Rosette the whole of the inside of the back wall as shown (**3**). With your hand and a knife, carefully raise the back section into position and join to sides E and F. Join I to the back of the castle H and O and Q at each side of the back.

6. Colour scheme for front.

3. Colour scheme for inside back.

Cut the wafer biscuits so that they fit along the sides of the cake at an angle as pictured.

Decorating the cake
Change the tube on the pale pink icing bag to a fine writer and pipe rambling lines over the wafers already on the cake and the cones. Position the cones on the cake. Change the tube to the star and rosette around the base of each cone to secure it in place. Dot silver balls over the cones and around the base of the cake. Cut sandwich flags to size and insert one into the top of each cone. Make a drawbridge by inserting the 2 chocolate matchsticks into either side of the entrance with wafers as the bridge. Fill the central courtyard with 100s and 1000s and attach the wafer roses and butterflies.

RAINBOW

Timing
2-3 hours to ice and
    decorate

Equipment
8 bowls for icing mixture
3 icing bags (minimum)
1 tube: stars
sharp knife
palette knife
cocktail stick or skewer
tracing paper
paint brush
13 in cake board

Ingredients
1 cake, 8×12 in (page
    11), cooled upside
    down
1 quantity of butter icing
    (page 12)
food colouring: royal
    blue, violet, grass
    green, orange,
    Christmas red, yellow
2 tablespoons marzipan
    (page 16)
apricot glaze (optional –
    page 12)

Template
page 123. Instructions for
    making it on page 114.

Constructing the cake

Scale up and cut out the template. Place it on the cake and cut out the semi-circular shape. Prick out the colour bands with a cocktail stick, skewer or sharp knife. Lift on to the board.

Icing the cake

Divide the butter icing into 8 bowls and colour: ½ tablespoon royal blue mixed roughly to give a marbled effect, ½ tablespoon violet, 1 tablespoon royal blue and violet mixed together, 1½ tablespoons royal blue, 5 tablespoons grass green, 1½ tablespoons yellow, 2 tablespoons orange, 3 tablespoons red. Begin by flat icing the central semi-circle in the blue and white marbled icing. Put the violet icing into a bag fitted with the star tube and following the pricked out lines and using the photograph or the template as a guide, rosette 2 rows for the violet colour band. Using a clean bag and tube for each colour continue icing 2 rows for each colour band. Rosette the sides of the cake with the red icing and lastly rosette the grass at the base of the cake.

Decorating the cake

Colour the marzipan with the green food colouring and roll it out. Using the template, cut out the trees and lift them on to the cake with a palette knife. With a paint brush or skewer dipped in blue food colour, paint on the birds in the sky.

BALLET SHOES

BALLET SHOES

Timing
2-2½ hours to ice and
    decorate

Equipment
2 bowls for icing mixture
2 icing bags
3 tube: fine and thick
    writer, stars
palette knife
sharp knife
tracing paper
cocktail stick or skewer
13 in cake board

Ingredients
1 cake, 8×12 in (page
    11), cooled upside
    down
1 quantity of white
    butter icing (page 13)
food colouring: rose pink
apricot glaze (optional –
    page 12)

Template
page 123. Instructions
    for making it on page
    114.

Decoration
2¼ yards pale satin
    ribbon

1

Constructing the cake
Scale up and cut out the template. Place it on the cake and cut out around the shoes as accurately as possible. Prick through the shoe outlines with a cocktail stick, skewer or sharp knife. Carefully cut away the front edges of the shoe, shaping to give a curved effect (**1**). Lift the cake on to the cake board.

Icing the cake
Divide the butter icing into 2 bowls and colour: 3 tablespoons very pale pink, 12 tablespoons rose. If possible, try to match the rose colour of the icing to your ribbon. Add colouring slowly; the shoes should be a delicate pink.

With pale pink icing, flat ice the centre of the sole. Add a little more pink to the icing you have left over, and with this, flat ice the inner sides of the shoe. This is reasonably difficult and you may decide to flat ice the whole of the inside of the shoe with the pale pink. It is also difficult to rosette in between the shoes at the front; smooth a little icing on with a wet palette knife before you start with the icing bag.

Put the rose icing into a bag fitted with the thick writer tube and pipe around the rim of the shoes. Change to the star tube and rosette the shoes. Change to a fine writer and pipe in the lines outlining the sole, the seams and the bow at the front.

Decorating the cake
Add the ribbon just before serving the cake as the fat does seep through.

Timing
3-4 hours to ice and
   decorate, though the
   marzipan should be
   left to dry out on the
   cakes for about 2-4
   days.

Equipment
sharp knife
paint brush
pin or needle
tracing paper
16 in cake board

Ingredients
1 rich fruit cake, baked
   in a 11×3×3 in loaf
   tin (page 11),
4 lb marzipan (page 16)
4 lb or 36 tablespoons of
   fondant (page 16)
food colouring:
   Christmas red, yellow,
   grass green, sky blue,
   orange, black (or
   colours of your choice)
apricot glaze (page 12)

Template
page 124. Instructions for
   making it on page 114.
   The letters have been
   reproduced to the
   actual size needed for
   these blocks of cake.

BLOCKS FOR A BABY

Constructing the cakes
Cut the cake into 4 cubes measuring 2½ in. Try to be as accurate as possible so that the cubes all look an equal size. Brush with apricot glaze.

Decorating the cakes
Roll out the marzipan to about ¼ in thickness. Cut into squares and fit to the sides of the cakes. Ideally this should be done 2-4 days in advance so that the marzipan can dry out before the fondant is placed on top.

Roll out the fondant and cut it into squares to fit the sides. Brush the marzipan lightly with apricot glaze and lay the fondant in place, making sure the edges join neatly.

Scale up the templates for the block picture designs. The letters have been reproduced to the correct size for the blocks. Simply trace them off the page. Place the designs on the blocks and prick through with a pin to transfer the design to the fondant. Choose the colours, and paint in the pictures, cleaning the brush before each change of colour.

Additional hints
You could easily make some pictures of your own for the blocks. Painting them is time-consuming but enjoyable and worth the effort.

EASTER EGG

EASTER EGG

Timing
1½ hours to ice and
   decorate

Equipment
2 bowls for icing mixture
1 icing bag
3 tube: medium writer
palette knife
sharp knife
tracing paper
13 in cake board

Ingredients
1 cake, 8×12 in (page
   11), cooled upside
   down
1 quantity of butter icing
   (page 12)
2½ tablespoons yellow
   marzipan (page 16)
food colouring: rose,
   yellow (if the
   marzipan is not yellow
   enough), cocoa
   powder
apricot glaze (optional –
   page 12)

Constructing the cake

Scale up and cut out the template. Place on
the cake and cut out around the egg shape.
Lift the cake on to the board. Shave the edges
of the cake to make a rounded, and more
egg-like shape.

Icing the cake

Divide the butter icing into 2 bowls and
colour: 2 tablespoons soft pink, 13
tablespoons light brown. Flat ice the sides
and top of the cake with the brown.
Dipping the palette knife in water, smooth
the icing up from the sides and over on to
the top, retaining a rounded edge to the
cake. Repeat until the cake looks smooth.

Roll out the marzipan. (Colour yellow first
if the natural colour of the marzipan is not
intense enough.) Cut a strip 12 in long and
1½ in wide and lay it diagonally across the
cake, using the photograph as a guide. Roll
out the leftover marzipan and cut a strip 8
in long and 1½ in wide. Fold the sides
under and pinch the centre to make a bow.
Place the bow on the marzipan ribbon.

Fill the icing bag with pink icing and fit the
medium writer tube and carefully pipe in the
lines along the ribbon and bow. Dot the area
of the cake above the diagonal ribbon. Add
the decorations.

Additional hints

If the cake is being made for Easter, there are
many pretty things in the shops at this time.
Little wooden rabbits, chicks, chocolate
rabbits, sugar eggs, nests and so on would
complement this simple cake idea.

BIRTHDAY PRESENT

Timing
3 hours to ice and
  decorate

Equipment
4 bowls for icing mixture
tape measure
stainless steel cutters for
  moon and star shapes
cocktail stick or skewer
palette knife
tissue paper or kitchen
  towels
paint brush
16 in cake board

Ingredients
2 rich fruit cakes, 8×12
  in (page 11)
3½ lb marzipan (page
  16)
5 lb fondant (page 16)
food colouring: violet,
  royal blue, lemon
  yellow, Christmas red
apricot glaze (optional –
  page 12)

Decorations
coloured thread for the
  label

Constructing the cake

Place one cake on the cake board and lightly brush the top with apricot glaze. Roll out a piece of marzipan 8×12 in and ¼ in thick. Place on top of the cake and brush the marzipan with a little more apricot glaze before placing the second cake on top. Brush the sides of the cake with apricot glaze.

Icing the cake

Roll out the rest of the marzipan to ¼ in thick and, measuring each area as you go, cover the 4 sides of the cake. Cut another strip of marzipan 1 in wide and long enough to go right around the rim of the cake. You may like to do this in four pieces. This will give the lid effect on the parcel. Roll out and cut the remaining marzipan to cover the top of the cake after first brushing with apricot glaze. Leave the cake to dry out for 2-4 days before decorating with fondant.

Colour 3 lb of the fondant with violet and royal blue food colouring to get a rich purple as shown in the photograph. Brush the sides of the marzipan-covered cake with apricot glaze and measure the depth from the cake board to just below the double layer of marzipan that represents the rim of the box. Roll out the purple fondant and cut 4 pieces for the lower half of the sides and 4 pieces for the rim. Place on the cake. Brush the top of the cake with the apricot glaze and roll out the remainder of the purple fondant for the top. Either roll the fondant over a rolling pin to lift it on to the cake or cut into 4 pieces and place on top of the cake. The cut lines will be concealed by the ribbon.

Colour 2 tablespoons of the fondant lemon yellow and take a further 2 tablespoons of the white. Roll out. With the stainless steel cutters, cut out the desired number of stars and moons. Apply a drop of apricot glaze to each one and place on the cake, using the photograph as a guide.

Roll out 2 tablespoons of the white fondant and cut out the label. With a skewer or cocktail stick, make a hole in the label and thread the coloured thread through it. You can write on a message with food colouring and a paint brush. Put to one side.

Colour the remaining fondant Christmas red. Roll out and cut 4 strips 1½ in wide to fit over the parcel. Place these on the cake. To make the bow, roll out the red offcuts and cut a strip 10×1½ in. Curve the cut ends into the middle point to make a bow. Support the bow with tissue until set. From the remnants cut a centre piece for the bow and 2 end pieces. Cut a triangle from one end of each end piece and place on the cake as shown in the photograph. Place the label on the cake.

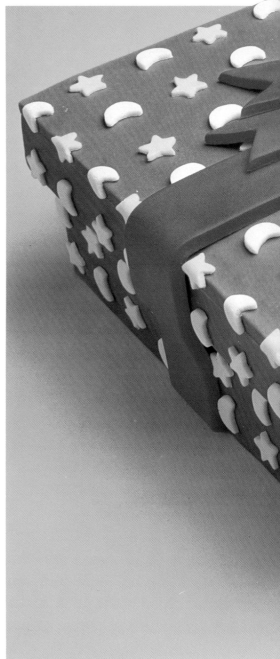

EASTER BASKET

Timing
3-4½ hours to ice and
   decorate (the cane
   handle can be made in
   advance)

Equipment
3 bowls for icing mixture
3 icing bags
4 tube: ribbing, nut
   brown 5, Ateco 96,
   Ateo 47
   (ribbon)palette knife
sharp knife
tracing paper
13 in cake board

Ingredients
½ cake mixture, baked
   in a 6×3×3 in loaf tin
   (page 11)
1 quantity of butter icing
   (page 12)
food colouring: light
   beige (cocoa with a
   little lemon colour),
   medium beige (cocoa
   and lemon), dark
   beige (more intense
   cocoa and lemon)
apricot glaze (optional –
   page 12)

Decoration
24 in rattan cane
60 in lapping cane
string
2 small tacks
flowers or eggs
An alternative handle
   could be made with a
   wire coat hanger
   covered with 2½
   tablespoons of
   marzipan (page 16)

The handle
Pour boiling water over the rattan cane and
soak for 3 hours. Bend, cut to fit the cake and
tie firmly across the centre with string to
hold it in a looped shape. Leave to dry and
whittle ends to a point (**1**). Cut the lapping
cane in half and starting from either end of
the handle, wrap both pieces around the
handle. Secure each end with a small tack.

Constructing the cake
The cake will take longer to cook in a loaf
tin so test with a skewer. The cake should
have a slightly narrower base. Accentuate
this by shaving carefully round the base of
the cake with a sharp knife. Cut out a ¼ in
hollow in the top of the cake. Lift the cake
on to the board.

Icing the cake
Divide the butter icing into 3 bowls and
colour: 8 tablespoons light beige, 3
tablespoons medium beige, 4 tablespoons
dark beige. Roughly flat ice the cake with
the light beige icing. Put the dark beige
into an icing bag fitted with the ribbing
tube and pipe on the basket uprights
around the cake about every 1 in or so. Put
to one side. Change to a clean bag filled
with light beige and the Ateco 96 tube and
pipe on the border at the base of the cake.
Using the Ateco 47 (ribbon) tube and
medium beige, begin the basket weave by
piping broken horizontal lines around the
cake. Pipe over one upright and stop at the
next and so on. Start at the base and work
up to the rim. Use the photograph as a
guide. Stop about 1¼ in from the top.

Change back to dark beige and with the
ribbing tube pipe in the diagonals on the
rim. Begin at the top, pipe the line and before
touching the tube tip to the cake, lift the bag
up. This will give the diagonal curve. Repeat
all round the rim. Fill in the basket, icing the
diagonal lines in the opposite direction (**2**).

Decorating the cake
Insert the cane handle; don't remove the
string. Make a piped base for the handle on
the outer rim at either end with medium
beige and the Ateco 47 tube. Place the
flowers or eggs in the hollow of the basket.

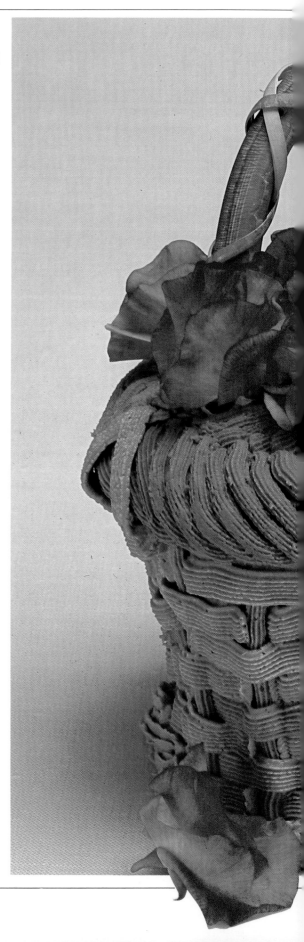

EASTER BASKET

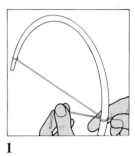

1

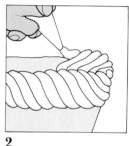

2

VALENTINE HEART

Timing
2 hours to ice and
    decorate

Equipment
1 bowl for icing mixture
2 icing bags
3 tubes: star, medium
    and fine writers
palette knife
cocktail stick or skewer
ruler
stainless steel cutters for
    the heart shapes
sharp knife
tissue paper
paint brush
13 in cake board

Ingredients
1 cake, 8×8 in (page 11),
    cooled upside down
1 quantity of white
    butter icing (page 13)
1 tablespoon fondant
    (page 16)
food colouring:
    Christmas red
apricot glaze (optional –
    page 12)

Template
page 125. Instructions
    for making it on page
    114.

Constructing the cake
Scale up and cut out the template. Place on the cake and cut out around the heart shape. Lift the cake on to the board.

Icing the cake
Put ½ tablespoon of the butter icing into a bowl and colour red; the rest leave white. Flat ice the top of the cake with the white, smoothing out to the sides. Fill the icing bag with the rest of the white and with the star tube rosette around the sides. With a cocktail stick or skewer and a ruler held above the cake, prick in a dot at 1 in intervals around the edge of the cake starting at the bottom tip. Change the tube to the medium writer and pipe around the top of the cake in semi-circles using the dots as a guide. Pipe in matching semi-circles over the rosettes on the outside. Pipe a small dot at every other join. With a cocktail stick, prick on the words "Be mine". Put the red icing in a clean bag and with the fine writer tube, pipe on the message.

Decorating the cake
Colour the fondant red and roll out. With a heart-shaped stainless steel cutter, or freehand if you feel confident, cut out 21 hearts and place them on the cake – one at every other semi-circle join and 1 on the sides below the piped dots. From the rest of the fondant, mould the flowers (page 17) and roll a long piece for the ribbon. Place the fondant posy on the cake.

Additional hints
The inscription could of course be changed. Sugar or wafer biscuits could be used in place of the fondant, or even real flowers. Heart tins are available in the shops and are a useful shape to have. This cake could easily be adapted for a wedding anniversary.

HALLOWE'EN COFFIN

Timing
2-3 hours to ice and
  decorate

Equipment
3 bowls for icing mixture
3 icing bags
2 tubes: star, ribbon
palette knife
sharp knife
paint brush
13 in cake board

Ingredients
2 cakes, 8×12 in (page
  11), cooled upside
  down
1½ quantity of white
  butter icing (page 13)
1 tablespoon fondant
  (page 16)
food colouring:
  Christmas red, black,
  gold food paint
apricot glaze (optional –
  page 12)

Template
page 125. Instructions
  for making it on page
  114.

Decoration
skeleton

Constructing the cake

Scale up the template, marking the inner line too, and cut it out. Place the template on one of the cakes and cut out around the outer line. Lift the cake on to the cake board. Place the template on the other cake and cut around the outer line, then cut out the central area up to the inner line.

Icing the cake

Divide the butter icing into 3 bowls and colour: 1 tablespoon white, 8 tablespoons red, 10 tablespoons black. Flat ice the top of the base with red. Place the cut-out top section on to the base and flat ice the inner sides red. Put the remainder of the red in an icing bag fitted with a star tube and rosette around the line where the base meets the sides of the coffin. With black icing, flat ice the sides of the cake. Smooth up and over to the top so that the rosettes will be piped on to flat icing. This gives a neater look. Put the rest of the black icing in a clean bag fitted with a star tube and rosette around the top and the sides of the coffin using the photograph as a guide. Using a clean bag, the ribbon tube and white icing, carefully pipe the frill around the top of the coffin.

Decorating the cake

Roll out the fondant and with a sharp knife cut out 6 tiny handles and a scroll for the RIP from the template. Dip the paint brush into the gold food colouring and paint on the letters and the scroll work. Paint the handles too. Place the handles on the cake. Add flowers, the skeleton and other decorations.

Additional hint

We have done this cake for Hallowe'en which is becoming a more popular festival. There are many different symbols to use – bats, cats, pumpkins.

With this cake there is quite a bit of wastage which could be turned into spider cakes. Cut the remaining cake into shapes – don't worry about them being even – and flat ice them white. Add a little black to the white to make a greyish colour, put into a clean icing bag fitted with a fine writer tube and pipe on a spider's web.

HALLOWE'EN COFFIN

HAMBURGER PARTY

Timing
3 hours to ice and
    decorate

Equipment
7 bowls for icing mixture
1 icing bag
1 tube: thick writer
palette knife
sharp knife
tracing paper
13 in cake board

Ingredients
1 round cake, 8 in in
    diameter (page 11),
    either bake in 2
    sandwich tins or a
    deep tin. Cool one
    cake right side up to
    retain the rise.
1½ quantities of butter
    icing (page 12)
12 tablespoons marzipan
    (page 16)
food colouring: grass
    green, lemon yellow,
    Christmas red, black,
    bun brown (cocoa and
    egg yellow),
    hamburger (cocoa,
    black and Christmas
    red)
apricot glaze (optional –
    page 12)

Decoration
sesame seeds
red napkins

HAMBURGER PARTY

Constructing the cake
Shape the top half of your cake with a sharp knife to give it a more bun-like look. If you have made one cake, split it through crosswise. Lift the flat base on to the board which has been decorated with red napkins.

Icing the cake
Divide the butter icing into 3 bowls and colour: 15 tablespoons bun brown, 2 tablespoons red, the remainder leave white. This will be used to fill the centre of the bun. Flat ice the sides of the base of the hamburger with bun brown. On another board or a baking tray, flat ice the sides of the top of the hamburger too. Add a little more cocoa to the bun brown to deepen slightly, and flat ice the top. Scatter sesame seeds on the top.

Decorating the cake
Divide the marzipan into 4 bowls and colour: 3 tablespoons green, ½ tablespoon lemon yellow, 5½ tablespoons hamburger brown, 3 tablespoons egg yellow. Using your fingers to push the marzipan into shape, put on the green around the edge of the bun for lettuce. Mix in a little lemon yellow. This should look uneven and rather curled in places to resemble lettuce leaves. Put the red butter icing into an icing bag fitted with the thick writer tube and pipe on the tomato ketchup over the lettuce to look as though it is oozing out.

With your fingers, put the hamburger brown marzipan around the edges a little way in from the lettuce. The effect should be much the same all round the cake. Roll out the egg yellow marzipan and cut it into 4 triangles. Place a triangle at each corner of the hamburger. With the white butter icing, fill the centre of the hamburger. Carefully lift the top on to the base, and sprinkle it with sesame seeds.

We have not filled the cake with marzipan; it would be too sweet for most palates. Real whipped cream could be used instead of butter icing or pieces of cake could fill in the space.

COMING-OF-AGE CRACKER

Timing
2-3 hours to ice and decorate though the marzipan should be left to dry out for about 2-4 days

Equipment
2 bowls for icing mixture
sharp knife
ravioli cutter
kitchen paper towels
tracing paper
14 in cake board

Ingredients
1 rich fruit cake, made in a 12×3×3 in loaf tin (page 11)
7 tablespoons marzipan (page 16)
14 tablespoons fondant (page 16)
food colour: royal blue
apricot glaze (page 12)

Template
page 125. Instructions for making it on page 114.

Decoration
white paper doyley
the number 18 in silver paper
20 in white satin ribbon

Constructing the cake

Scale up the template and cut out the 3 template pieces. Put to one side. With a sharp knife, shape the cake. Mark a point 4 in in from either end of the cake and insert a cocktail stick at both points. This marks the central section. Cut down from the end toward the cocktail stick (**1**) and remove a thin wedge of cake. With the knife, round the top of the central section and the two ends. Brush the cake with apricot glaze and lift on to the board. Roll out the marzipan and cover the entire cake, finishing with the two vertical outside edges.

Decorating the cake

Colour 2 tablespoons of the fondant the palest blue. Roll out the rest of the white fondant and using the template cut out the central strip; measure the cake first to make sure it is going to be coverred by a strip 4×8 in. Brush the marzipan lightly with apricot glaze and place the fondant over the central section of the cake, wrapping it round. Cut 2 end pieces to cover the outside edges. Roll out the fondant again and cut out 2 frills from the template (**2**). Have some kithen towels nearby and place a frill over either end of the cake, gathering the ends softly. Pad the folds with kitchen towels to support the folds until the fondant is dry.

Roll out the blue fondant and cut 4 strips, ½ in wide and 8 in long, and 2 long strips, ¼ in wide and 12 in long. Cut along one straight edge with a ravioli cutter or cut the zigzags by hand with a sharp knife. Place 2 of the short strips at the joins where the central section meets the frill (use the photograph as a guide). Place a long strip on the ends of the frills – it does help to have a little apricot glaze under the thin strip so that it stays in place on the frill. Cut a doyley in half and shape it to fit round the neck at the junction of the frill and central section. Place it in position using the photograph as a guide. Place the remaining 2 wide strips upright against the flat wide strip on top of the doyley. Cut a piece of ribbon for the centre and position the numerals on it. Remove the kitchen towels once the fondant is dry.

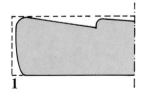

1

2

CHRISTMAS STOCKING

CHRISTMAS STOCKING

Timing
2½ hours to ice and
  decorate

Equipment
5 bowls for icing mixture
3 icing bags
2 tubes: star, ribbing
palette knife
sharp knife
cocktail stick or skewer
paint brush
tracing paper
14 in cake board

Ingredients
1 cake, 8×12 in (page 11)
  cooled upside down
4 tablespoons fondant
  (page 16)
food colouring:
  Christmas red, grass
  green, silver or gold
  food colouring
apricot glaze (page 12)

Template
page 126. Instructions
  for making it on page
  114.

Decoration
sugar Father Christmas

Constructing the cake

Scale up and cut out the template. Place it on the cake and cut out around the 2 shapes. Prick through the heel and stripe lines with a cocktail stick, skewer or sharp knife. Lift the 2 pieces on to the board and join together with a little butter icing.

Icing the cake

Divide the butter icing into 3 bowls and colour: 5 tablespoons red, 4 tablespoons green, 6 tablespoons white. Flat ice the top of the heel and the top inside part of the stocking, smoothing out to the edges. Put the red icing in a bag fitted with the ribbing tube and pipe in the ribbing at the top of the stocking, piping a line round the white section and finishing with a bow at the back. Change the tube to a star and rosette the rest of the red area on the stocking, using the photograph and template as a guide. Continue rosetting the cake using clean bags and the star tube with the white and the green. Mark in the stitching lines on the heel with a cocktail stick or skewer.

Decorating the cake

Divide the fondant into 2 bowls and colour: 2 tablespoons green, 1 tablespoon red, and the rest leave white. Roll out the green and using the templates, cut out 2 tiny Christmas trees and 8 holly leaves. From the red make the large bow by moulding the shapes with your fingers. Make the knot with the base of a tube. Roll out somne tiny pieces of red for the berries and roll a thin strip between your fingers for the bow on the holly wreath. Roll out the white and cut out 3 bells and 2 stars. Put the fondant decorations on the cake, using the photograph as a guide. With a paint brush dipped in gold or silver food colouring, paint the stars and the bells. Remove these before eating, as the food paint is inedible. Put the sugar Father Christmas inside the holly wreath and make the marks on the large bow with a knife.

CHRISTMAS TREE AND PRESENTS

Timing
1½ hours to ice and
  decorate the cake; 3
  hours to ice and
  decorate the presents
The marzipan will need
  2-4 days to dry out
  and the first icing
  needs 24 hours to set.

  Equipment
2 bowls for icing mixture
1 small airtight container
1 icing bag
1 tube: fine writer
palette knife
stainless steel cutters for
  the star shapes
sharp knife
14 in cake board
paint brush

Ingredients
1 rich fruit cake, 8×12 in
  (page 11)
1 quantity of royal icing
  (page 13)
16 tablespoons marzipan
  (page 16)
6 tablespoons fondant
  (page 16)
food colouring:
  Christmas red, grass
  green, choice of colour
  for the presents
apricot glaze (page 12)

  Template
page 126. Instructions
  for making it on page
  114.

  Decoration
silver balls
silver candle holders
sugar angels, bells,
  wreaths
choir boy
red robin

Constructing the cake
Scale up and cut out the template. Place the template on the cake and cut out around the tree shape and cut the presents from the waste cake. Brush the cakes with apricot glaze. Roll out the marzipan and cover the tree and presents with it. Cover with a cloth and leave to dry for 2-4 days. Lift the tree cake on to the board.

Icing the cake
Put 4 tablespoons of the royal icing in an airtight container in the fridge and colour the remainder green. Roughly flat ice the cake with the green, using the palette knife to give a bushy effect. Leave the cake to dry for 24 hours.

From the stored icing, colour 3 tablespoons dark green and 1 tablespoon red. Put the dark green into a bag fitted with a fine writer and pipe little J shapes all over the cake using the photograph as a guide. Pipe the curved lines for the garlands by going back and forth across the cake. Now pipe a wavy line over top of the first.

Decorating the cake
Dot silver balls along the garland. Put a little icing on the back of the sugar decorations and place them on the tree. Insert the candle holders and candles.

Decorating the presents
Divide the fondant into 1½ tablespoon amounts and colour with your choice of food colouring. Brush the presents lightly with apricot glaze. Roll out the fondant and cover the shapes.
Top: White fondant mixed with a little red gives it a marbled effect and then we covered it with stars cut from red fondant.
Left: Black fondant covers the cake, white stars are placed on it and red butter icing is piped around the lid and to form a bow.
Right: Green butter icing is piped on to red fondant.
Bottom: Uncoloured fondant covers the cake and tiny holly leaves are painted on with green food colouring. The ribbon is piped on with butter icing and a fine writer tube.

HOUSE-WARMING CAKE

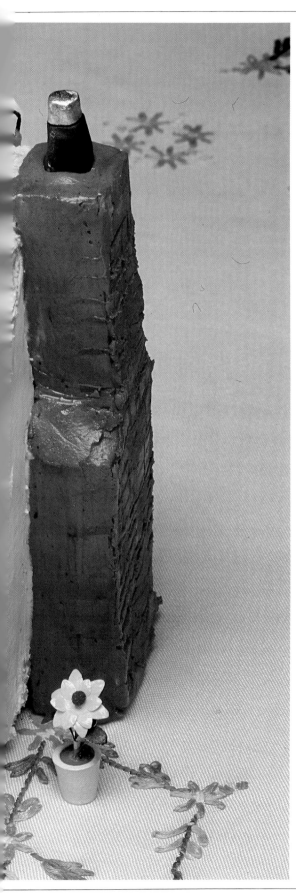

Timing
3-4 hours to ice and
   decorate

Equipment
6 bowls for icing mixture
5 icing bags
4 tubes: ribbing, fine,
   medium and thick
   writers
palette knife
cocktail stick or skewer
fork
sharp knife
paint brush
tracing paper
13 in cake board

Ingredients
2 cakes, 8×12 in (page
   11) cooled upside
   down
2 quantities of butter
   icing (page 12)
food colouring: rose
   pink, royal blue, grass
   green, thatch (egg
   yellow and cocoa),
   brick (orange and
   cocoa), black, silver
   food colouring
1 tablespoon fondant or
   marzipan (page 16)
apricot glaze (page 12)

Template
page 126. Instructions
   for making it on page
   114.

Decoration
flower tubs and boxes
licorice all-sorts for the
   doorstep

Constructing the cake
Scale up and cut out the template twice. One
template has the chimney shape cut from it.
Place on the cakes and cut the 6 shapes.
Using butter icing to join the pieces of cake
together, place cake A on the board. Place
cakes B and C on top of it. With a sharp
knife, cut a triangular section off cakes D and
E to give a sloping roof shape. Use the off
cuts for the top of the roof (**1**).

Icing the cake
Divide the butter icing into 6 bowls and
colour: 14 tablespoons white, 10
tablespoons thatch, 2 tablespoons black, 1
tablespoon royal blue, ½ tablespoon green,
½ tablespoon pink. Flat ice the 4 sides of
the cake with the white icing up to the
edge of the roof. Roughly flat ice 3 sides of
the chimney in brick. Push it quite firmly
on to the side of the house – you will have
some finger marks on the icing, go over it
again with a wet palette knife. Mark out
rough brick lines on the chimney with a
knife blade. With the thatch-coloured
icing, roughly flat ice the roof, and build
out the dormer windows.

With a cocktail stick or skewer, mark out the
pattern across the top of the roof using the
photograph as a guide. With a fork, mark out
the thatching on the bottom part of the roof.
Put the rest of the thatch icing in a bag fitted
with the ribbing tube and pipe across the top
of the roof and the wavy pattern made by the
pricked mark. Pipe a thick line of thatch
icing over the back and front doors.

With a clean bag filled with blue icing and the
medium writer, pipe on the window frames
and the door. In another clean bag, with the
medium writer and the brick icing, pipe on
the windowsills. Dot a door handle in yellow
on both doors. Put the green icing in an icing
bag fitted with a fine writer tube and pipe on
the branches of the rambling rose. With pink
icing in a clean bag fitted with the ribbing
tube, rosette on the roses. Colour the
marzipan or fondant black and shape into a
cylinder for the chimney pot. Paint the top
part with the silver food colouring and allow
to dry. Stick a cocktail stick into the chimney
pot and insert it into the cake.

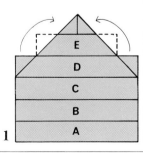

1

TOP HAT AND GLOVES

TOP HAT AND GLOVES

Timing
3 hours to ice and
    decorate

Equipment
2 bowls for icing mixture
palette knife
cocktail stick or skewer
sharp knife
kitchen paper towels
tracing paper
13 in cake board

Ingredients
2 cakes, 8×12 in (page
    11) cooled upside
    down
2 quantities of white
    butter icing (page 13)
12 tablespoons fondant
    (page 16)
food colouring: black
apricot glaze (page 12)

Template
page 1276. Instructions
    for making it on page
    114.

Constructing the cake
Scale up and cut out the template for the gloves, hat and rim. Cut out the oval hat shape from the cakes 4 times. Lift the first oval on to the cake board and join the other 3 to it with butter icing.

Icing the cake
Colour all the butter icing with a little black to make grey. Flat ice the cake beginning at the base and smoothing up to the top with a wet palette knife, making the edge where the sides meet the top as neat as possible. Flat ice the top, smoothing out to achieve a sharp, defined edge.

Decorating the cake
Roll out the fondant and lay the glove template on it. Cut out the shape carefully with a sharp knife. Prick through the lines of the fingers with a skewer or cocktail stick and then the lines of stitching on the glove. Collect up the remaining fondant and colour it with black to get the same grey colour as the butter icing on the hat. Roll out and cut out the rim template twice. Place the rim carefully around the base of the hat. Join by pressing the ends together with your fingers. Gently curve the rim upwards and hold in place with kitchen towels while the fondant sets. Colour what is left of the fondant with black. This method saves wastage. Roll out and cut a strip long enough to go around the hat and about 1 in wide. Cut another 1×2 in strip for the bow and wrap the band and bow around the hat. Place the gloves by the hat.

XYLOPHONE

XYLOPHONE

Timing
1½ hours to ice and
  decorate

Equipment
8 bowls for icing mixture
1 icing bag
1 tube: star
palette knife
sharp knife
tracing paper
cocktail stick or skewer
stainless steel cutters for
  moon, star and heart
  shapes
13 in cake board
Small biscuit cutter

Ingredients
1 cake, 8×12 in (page 11)
  cooled upside down
1 quantity of white
  butter icing (page 13)
10 tablespoons marzipan
  or fondant (page 16)
food colouring: sky blue,
  Christmas red,
  orange, yellow, violet,
  green, royal blue,
  maroon (red and
  blue)
apricot glaze (page 12)

Template
page 127. Instructions
  for making it on page
  114.

Decoration
string
toffee apple sticks
silver balls

Constructing the cake
Scale up and cut out the template. Place it on
the cake and cut out the 2 shapes. Place one
on top of the other on the cake board, joining
them with butter icing. With a sharp knife
shape the cake down towards one end (**1**).

Icing the cake
With the white butter icing, flat ice the top of
the cake, smoothing out to the sides. Fill the
icing bag with the rest of the white icing and
with the star tube, rosette the sides of the
xylophone.

Decorating the cake
Divide the marzipan or fondant for
colouring: 1 tablespoon each of maroon,
sky blue, orange, yellow, green, royal blue;
2 tablespoons each of the red and violet.
Roll out the marzipan or fondant and
using the templates, cut out the note plates
in the varying sizes, using the photograph
as a guide. From the fondant or marzipan
make tiny shapes with the stainless steel
cutters and place them on the top and
front of the cake.

The marzipan shapes can be made 1-2 days
in advance. Place the note plates on the cake
and put a silver ball at each end to represent
the screws. With the off cuts from the
coloured fondant, make up the rest of the
decoration.

Wheel base, wheels and string bead
Cut 4 large circles from the marzipan or
fondant (we have used red) with a small
glass or biscuit cutter and position these on
the sides of the cake. Divide the violet icing
into 4 and roll it in your hand to form a ball.
Place on a flat surface and gently press down
to flatten into a wheel. Join to the base.

Roll a piece of marzipan into a ball and with
a cocktail stick make a hole through it.
Thread a string through this marzipan ball
and attach to the cake by making a hole in
the cake with a skewer and pushing the
string into it. From the remaining marzipan,
make 2 hammers. Colour 2 toffee apple
sticks with food colouring and insert them
into the hammers.

1

TELEVISION SET

Timing
3 hours to ice and
    decorate

Equipment
3 bowls for icing mixture
1 icing bag
2 tubes: star, fine writer
palette knife
sharp knife
paint brush
tracing paper
13 in cake board

Ingredients
2 cakes, 8×12 in (page
    11) cooled upside
    down
2 quantities of white
    butter icing (page 13)
5 tablespoons marzipan
    (page 16)
food colouring:
    Christmas red, black,
    silver food paint
apricot glaze (page 12)

Template
page 127. Instructions
    for making it on page
    114.

Decoration
5×5 in photograph or
    picture backed with
    Bakewell paper to
    prevent it absorbing
    the butter

Constructing the cake
Scale up and cut out the template. Place it on one of the cakes and cut out around the 4 shapes. Take the tracing paper and place them on the second cake and cut out the same 4 shapes again. You will then have 2×A, 2×B, and 4×C. Scale up and cut out the marzipan template and put to one side. Lift A on to the cake board and place in an upright position; join the other piece A to it with a little butter icing. Centre the 2 pieces B at the back of A, to resemble the back of the television set. Then centre the 4 pieces C on to B (**1**).

Icing the cake
Flat ice the screen with the white butter icing, smoothing out to the sides. Put the remaining icing into the bag fitted with the star tube and rosette the rest of the cake.

Decorating the cake
Divide the fondant into 2 bowls and colour: 1 tablespoon black, 4 tablespoons grey. Remove 1 teaspoon from the marzipan to be coloured grey, and colour it with the red. Roll out the black, grey and red marzipan. From the grey, using the templates, cut out the frame of the screen, the handle, the button panel and the aerial knob. Paint the handle and the aerial knob with the silver food paint and leave to dry.

Dot the backed photograph or picture with a little butter icing and position on the cake. Place the pieces of the frame around the picture, attaching with a little icing. Position the panel alongside it. From the black marzipan, cut out the panel buttons and join on to the panel with icing. From the red cut out 2 panel buttons and put in place. Change the tube on the icing bag to the fine writer and pipe on the channel numbers. Place the handle and the aerial knob on the cake. As the silver food colouring is not edible, remove before the cake is eaten.

Additional hints
You could pipe a picture on to the screen or write the birthday message as though it were credits on the screen.

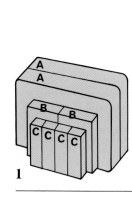

1

TELEVISION SET

GUITAR

Timing
2 hours to ice and
   decorate

Equipment
3 bowls for icing mixture
2 icing bags
2 tubes: star, fine writer
   cocktail stick or
   skewer
palette knife
sharp knife
tracing paper
16 in cake board

Ingredients
1 cake, 8×12 in (page 11)
   cooled upside down
1 quantity of butter icing
   (page 12)
   food colouring: cocoa
   powder, tan (orange
   with a little cocoa)
2½ tablespoons
   marzipan or fondant
   (page 16)
6 long strands of
   spaghetti
   apricot glaze (optional
   – page 12)

Template
page 128. Instructions
   for making it on page
   114.

Constructing the cake
Scale up and cut out the template. Place on the cake and cut around the 2 shapes. Prick through with a cocktail stick, skewer or sharp knife to mark the design lines on the cake – the curled design at the base of the guitar, the circle and the extension of the fret board. Lift the cakes on to the board and join the neck to the base with a little butter icing.

Icing the cake
Divide the butter icing into 3 bowls and colour: 3 tablespoons dark brown, 8 tablespoons medium brown, 4 tablespoons white. Using the dark brown, flat ice the fret board, the circle and the curled decoration, smoothing with a wet palette knife. Put the white icing into a bag fitted with a star tube and rosette around the edges of the guitar, using the photograph as a guide. Change to a clean bag fitted with the star tube and filled with medium brown and rosette the rest of the guitar. Put the bag to one side.

Decorating the cake
Colour the marzipan or fondant tan and roll out. Place the template on the marzipan or fondant and cut out 5 frets, 1 circle and a longer fret. Make the 6 tuning keys by shaping rectangles of fondant or marzipan and squeezing the ends with your thumb to give the key shape. Place the frets, the longer fret and the circle on the cake using the photograph as a guide. Insert the tuning keys. You may find it easier to join the keys to the cake by inserting a cocktail stick into the key and the other end into the cake. Change the tube on the icing bag filled with the medium brown to a fine writer and pipe the decorations on to the circle and the curled design. Pipe a little icing on to the top and bottom frets as an anchor for the strings. Break the spaghetti into even lengths and position on the cake.

PIANO

Timing
2-2½ hours to ice and
  decorate

Equipment
2 bowls for icing mixture
1 icing bag
1 tube: star
palette knife
sharp knife
tracing paper
fine paint brush
13 in cake board

Ingredients
2 cakes, 8×12 in (page
  11) cooled upside
  down
1½ quantities of butter
  icing (page 12)
6 tablespoons fondant
  (page 16)
2 tablespoons marzipan
  (page 16)food
  colouring: black,
  green, cocoa powder
apricot glaze (page 12)

Template
page 128. Instructions
  for making it on page
  114.

Decoration
wafer roses

Constructing the cake
Scale up and cut out the template. Place on the cakes and cut out twice. Lift the 2 pieces on to the board and join with a little butter icing. Cut out the keyboard section to the depth of one cake and round off the corners with a sharp knife.

Icing the cake
Divide the butter icing into 2 bowls and colour: 8 tablespoons very dark brown, 14 tablespoons light brown. Using the dark brown butter icing, flat ice the inside of the keyboard area. Flat ice the top of the piano, smoothing out to the sides. With the light brown and the star tube, rosette the sides of the piano.

Decorating the cake
Colour 1 tablespoon fondant black and 1 tablespoon light brown. Roll out the black, brown and the rest of the white fondant separately. Using the template, cut out the keyboard from the white. Place it on the cake and with a sharp knife mark the indents of the white keys, keeping them as even as possible. Cut out the black keys and place them over the white. From the light brown cut out the music stand and wedge it into the butter icing. It should stand at a slight angle. Cut out a music score freehand from the white fondant, and with a fine paint brush and black food colouring, paint on the score. Place it on the cake. Do more music sheets if necessary.

Music stool
Using a piece of leftover cake, cut out a music stool, either from the template or your own shape. Colour the marzipan brown and roll out. Cover the cake with the marzipan. From any leftover fondant, you can make a cushion. We have coloured ours green. The stool can be covered in rosettes of butter icing instead of the marzipan. Place the wafer roses on the cake.

Additional hints
You could sit the cake on an appropriate score, such as *Happy Birthday*, or *The Anniversary Waltz*. The stool could be made out of chocolate bars joined together with butter icing and a tiny candelabrum could be placed on the cake to hold the candles.

TYPEWRITER

Timing
3 hours to ice and
    decorate

Equipment
6 bowls for icing mixture
2 icing bags
3 tubes: star, fine and
    medium writer
palette knife
cocktail stick or skewer
4 cocktail sticks
sharp knife
tracing paper
13 in cake board

Ingredients
1 cake, 8×12 in (page 11)
    cooled upside down
1 quantity of butter icing
    (page 12)
8 tablespoons fondant
    (page 16)
food colouring: black,
    Christmas red, lemon
    yellow, apricot glaze
    (page 12)

Template
page 128. Instructions
    for making it on page
    114.

Constructing the cake

Scale up and cut out the templates. Place the cake template on the cake and cut out A and B. Place section B on the cake board and mark the centre line across the cake. From this line cut the cake down at an angle. From section A cut 2 notches, one against one long edge and the other across the middle, using the template as a guide (**1**). Place A on top of the uncut piece of B (**2**).

Icing the cake

Divide the butter icing into 3 bowls and colour: 5 tablespoons white, 3 tablespoons lemon yellow, 7 tablespoons grey. Begin by flat icing the white areas on section A and the top central area of B where the keys will go. Put the yellow icing into a bag fitted with a star tube and rosette one row around the base of the cake and in the central V shaped section where A meets B. Change to a clean bag filled with grey icing and fitted with the star tube and rosette the rest of the cake. Change the tube to a medium writer and pipe on the lines around the white areas at the back of the typewriter and around the keyboard area. Put the icing bag to one side for later.

Decorating the cake

Divide the fondant into 3 bowls for colouring: ½ tablespoon red, 1 tablespoon white. Colour the rest black. Roll out the fondant ¼ in thick. From the black, using the template, cut the keyboard – 38 square keys (C), 2 rectangular pieces (D) and the long spacer (E); 2×F for the back of the typewriter, 2×G for the ends of the paper roll; 2×H for the locks. Shape the 2 large and 2 small knobs for the back in your hands from the leftover black.

Roll out the red and cut a triangle for the front on/off switch and 2 rectangles (D) for the tabs on the keyboard. Cut out I to place up beside the paper roll. From the white, roll out in your hand a 5 in roller. Place the blacck pieces G at either end and drop into the V section. Place all the fondant pieces on the cake using the photograph as a guide. Insert a cocktail stick into each of the 4 knobs and push them into the cake. Change the tube to the fine writer and pipe on the characters.

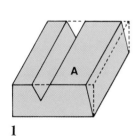

1

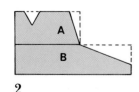

2

TYPEWRITER

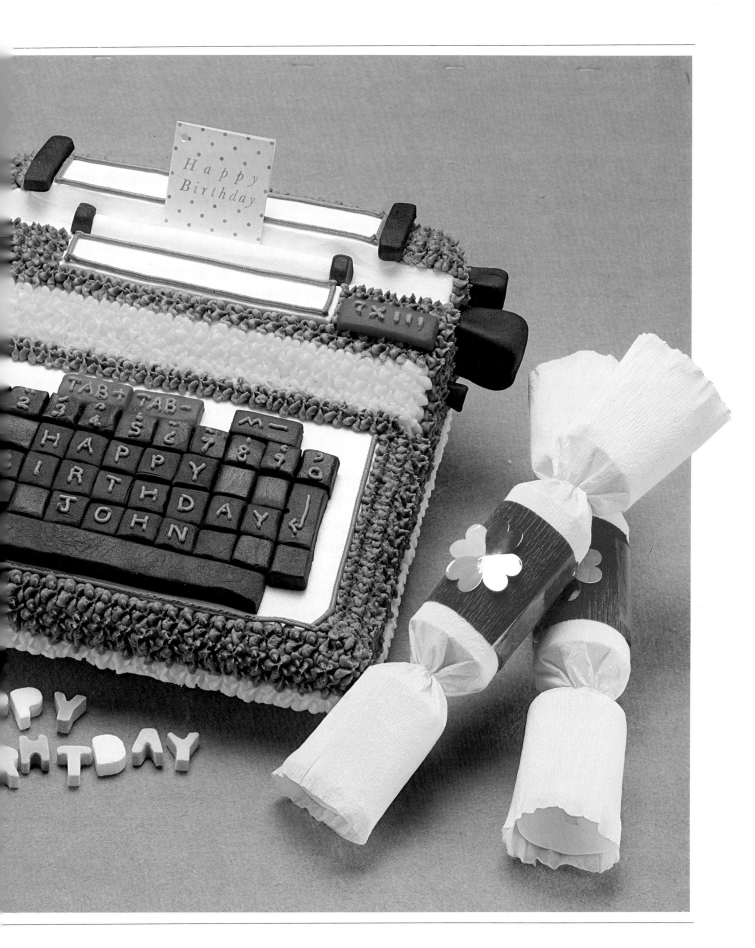

Templates

The shapes and internal design lines for the cakes in this book have been reproduced here to a smaller size. They have been drawn on a grid so that all you need do to reproduce them to the correct size is to draw the same shape on a larger grid. The grid here is made up of squares with ⅜ in sides. To enlarge the shapes to fit the 8×12 in cakes in this book, draw up a grid of squares with 1 in sides. Number the lines vertically and horizontally on both grids and make a small cross on the larger grid where the shape crosses a line on our drawing. Join up these crosses to get the finished shape. You can then trace this shape onto tracing paper, lay it on your cake, secure it with pins or cocktail stiks, and cut out around the outer lines. Any internal design lines will need to be pricked onto the cake too, or done freehand (see page 10).

If the template has letters on it which refer to the assembly instructions, make sure you write them on the tracing paper. Keep the pieces of cake labelled so that you do not lose track of them.

The areas coloured in dark pink are the shapes for the areas of fondant icing.

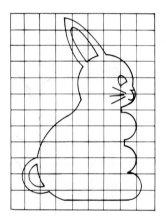

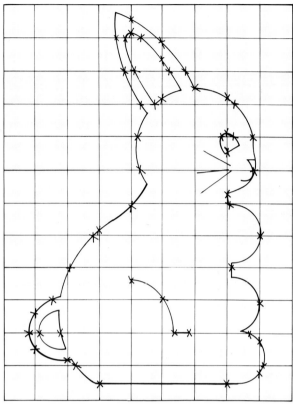

Soccer game – page 20

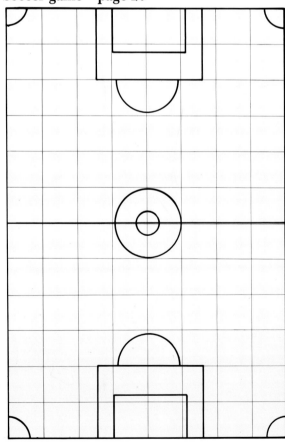

114

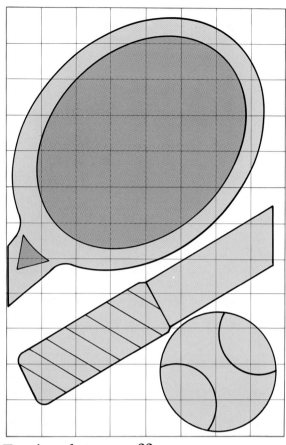

Tennis racket – page 22

Running shoe – page 24

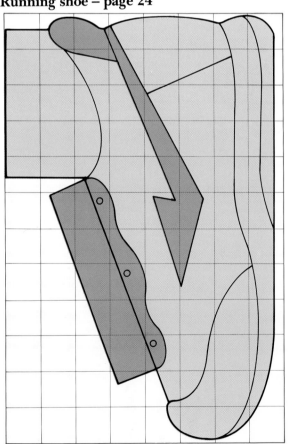

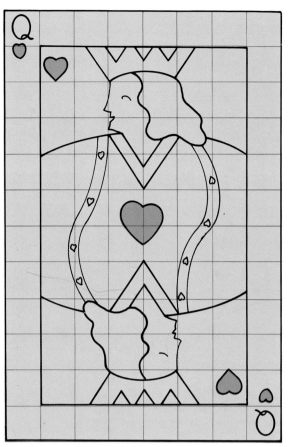

Playing card – page 26

Pink pig – page 30

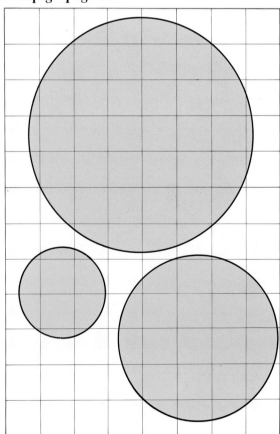

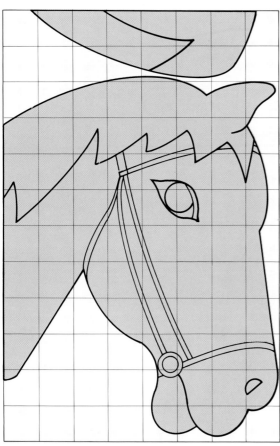

Horse's head – page 32

Koala bear – page 34

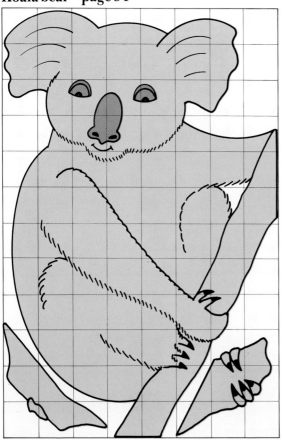

The cat – page 36

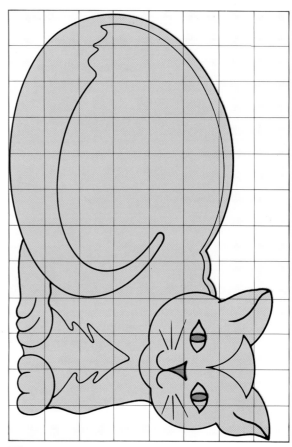

Three rabbits in bed – page 38

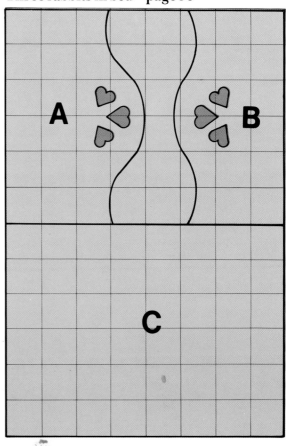

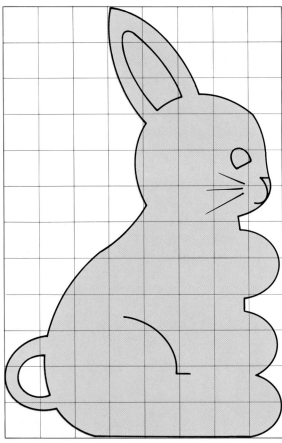

The rabbit – page 41

Freddie frog – page 42

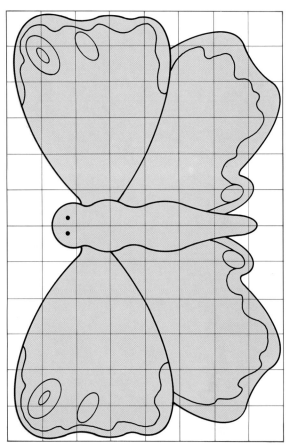

The butterfly – page 44

Racing car – page 46

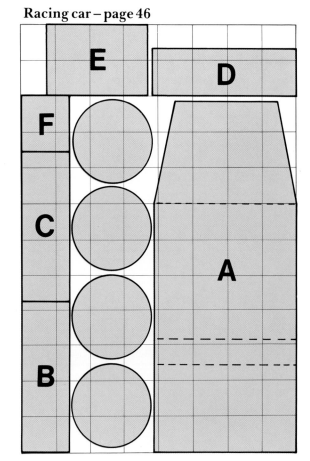

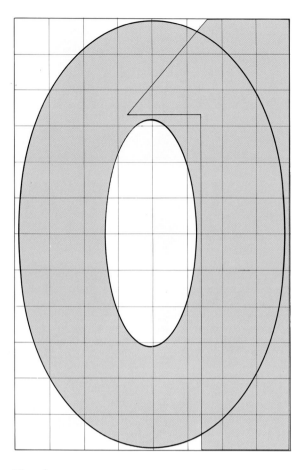

Numbers

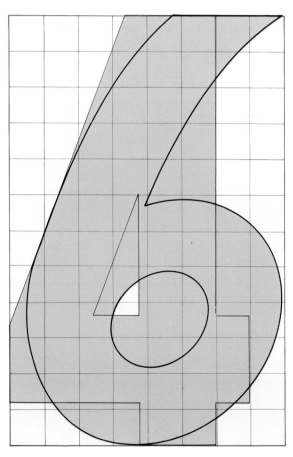

Racing track,   No. 8 – page 49

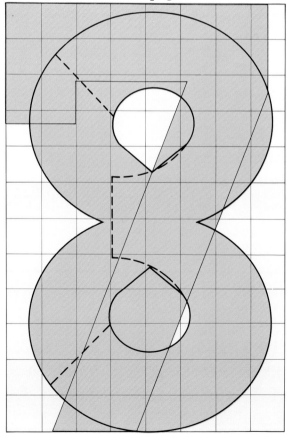

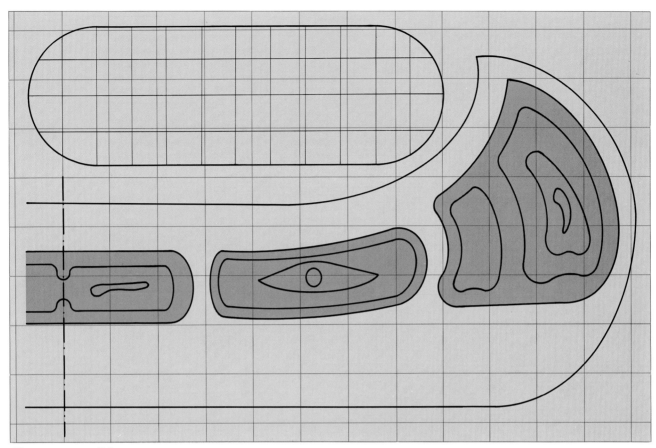

Canoe – page 50

Tank – page 54

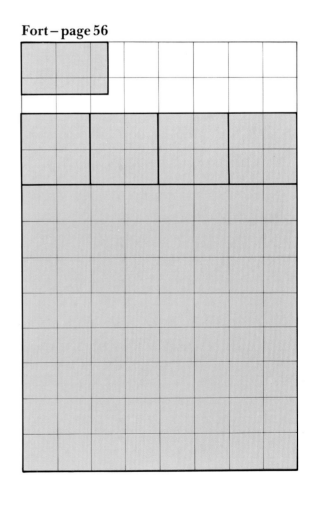

A

C   D

B   F

E

Fort – page 56

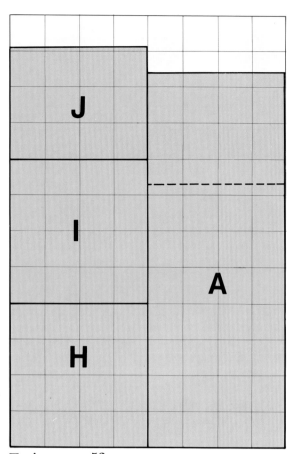

Train – page 52

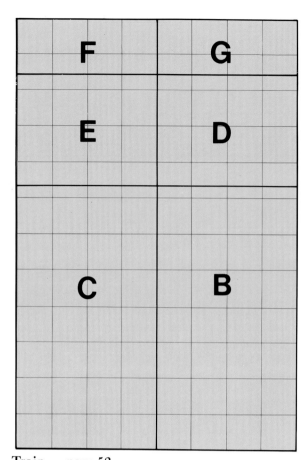

Train — page 52

Old woman who lived in a shoe – page 58

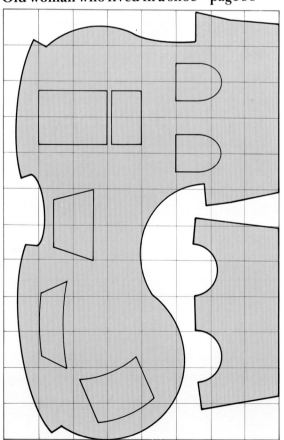

Incredible Hulk – page 60

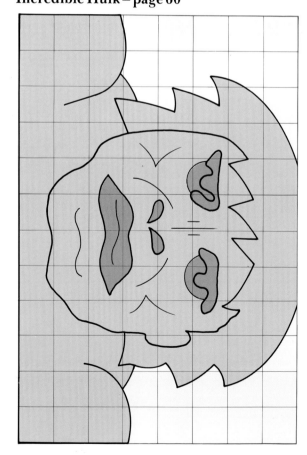

Wicked witch – page 64

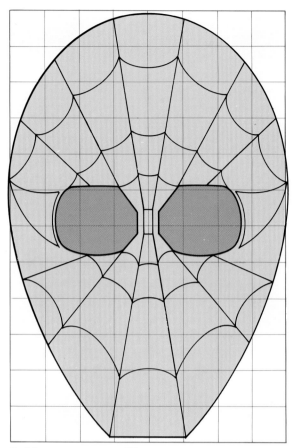

Spiderman – page 61

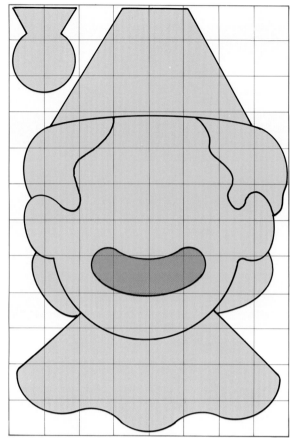

Clown face – page 68

Lady robot – page 66

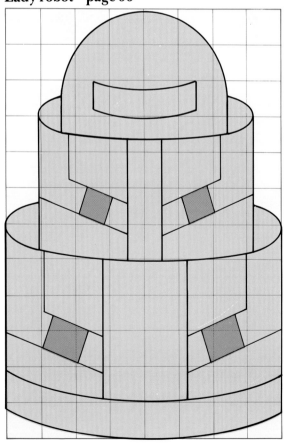

Treasure island – page 70

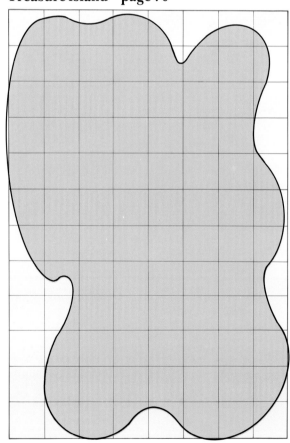

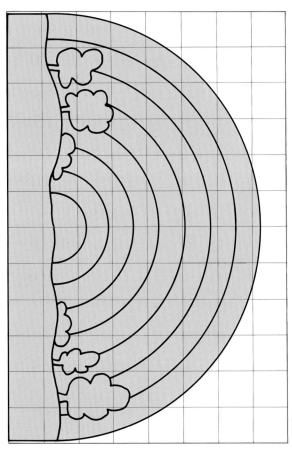

Rainbow – page 77

Fairy castle – page 74

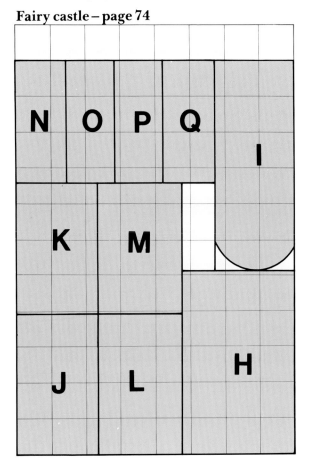

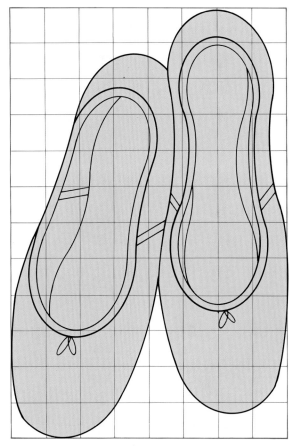

Ballet shoes – page 78

Fairy castle — page 74

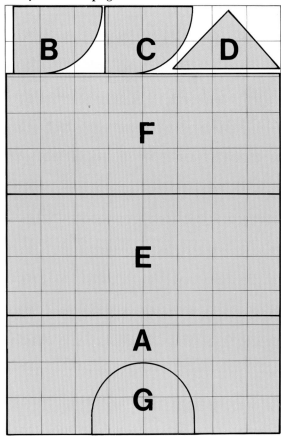

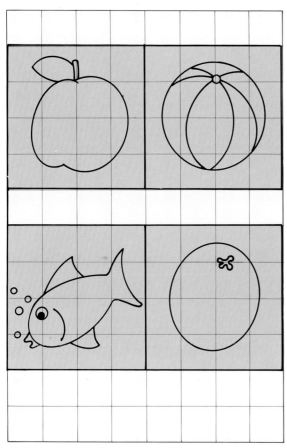

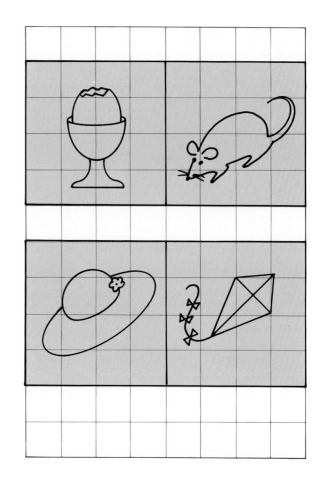

Blocks for a baby – page 80

abcdef
jklmno
stuvw

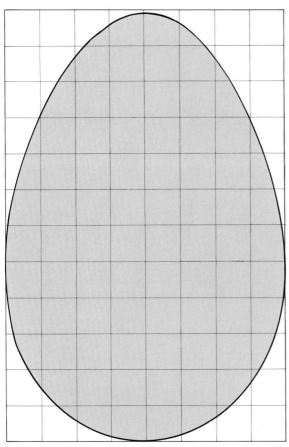

Easter egg – page 82

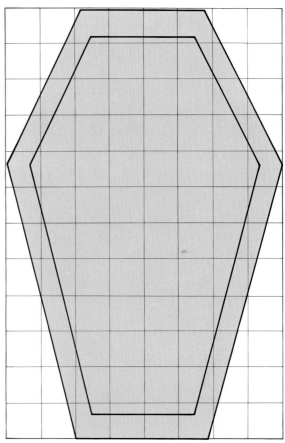

Hallowe'en coffin – page 90

Valentine heart – page 88

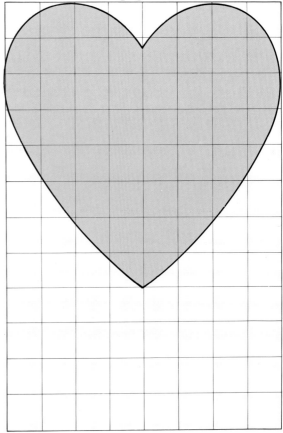

ghi
pqr
xyz

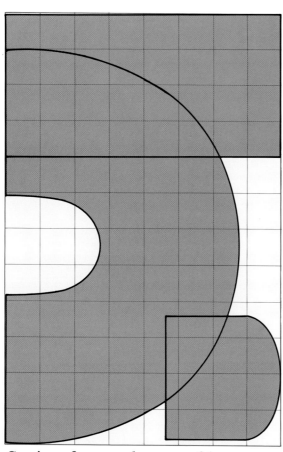

Coming-of-age cracker – page 94

Christmas stocking – page 96

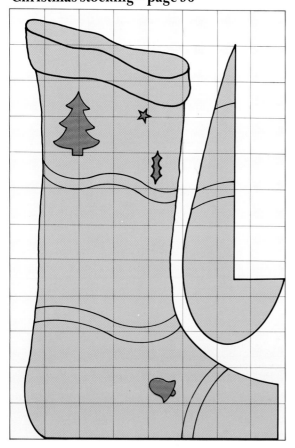

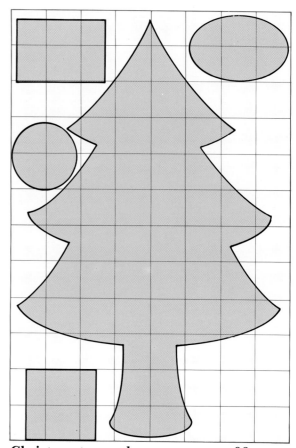

Christmas tree and presents – page 98

House-warming cake – page 100

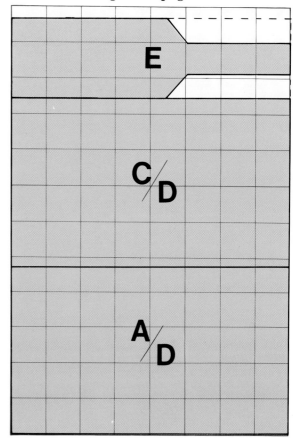

126

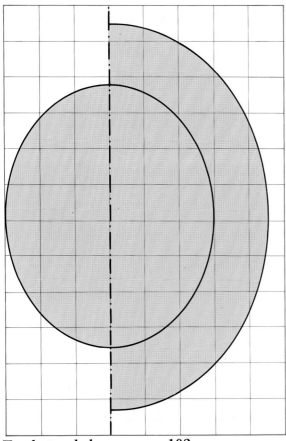

Top hat and gloves – page 102

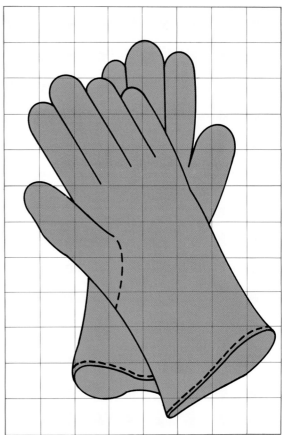

Top hat and gloves — page 102

Television set – page 106

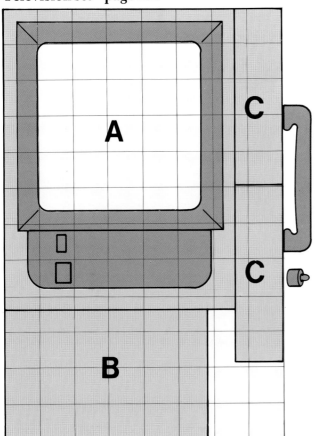

Xylophone – page 104

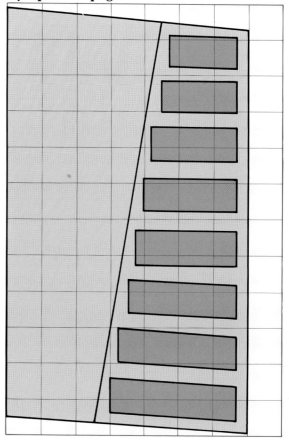

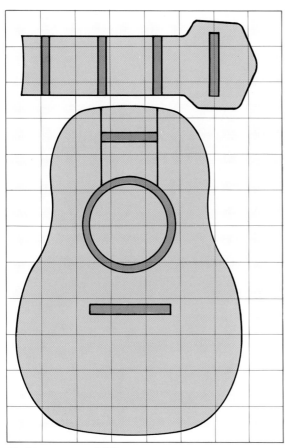

Guitar – page 108

Piano – page 110

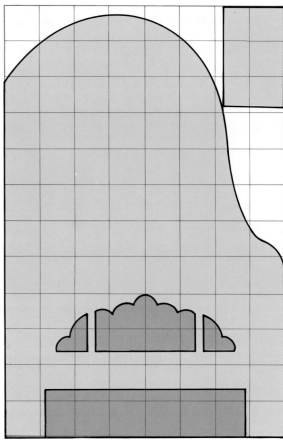

Typewriter – page 112

Typewriter — page 112

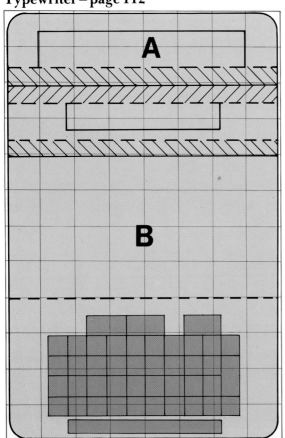

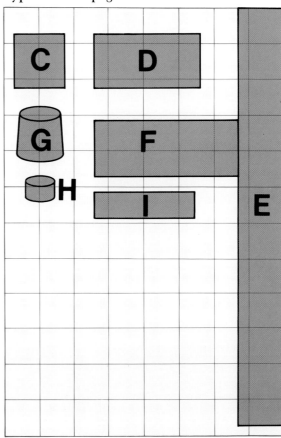